G000300469

CLV

Werner Gitt

# What About
# The Other Religions?

dₗv

Christliche
Literatur-Verbreitung e.V.
Postfach 110135 · 33661 Bielefeld

**The Author**, Prof Dr-Ing Werner Gitt was born in Raineck/East Prussia in 1937. In 1963 he enrolled at the 'Technische Hochschule Hannover' (Technical University Hanover) and in 1968 he completed his studies as "Diplom Ingenieur". Thereafter he worked as assistant an the Institute of Control Engineering at the 'Technische Hochschule Aachen' (TH Aachen). Following two years of research work, he received his doctorate in Engineering summa cum laude in 1970 together with the prestigious 'Borchers Medal' of the Technical University of Aachen. In 1971 Werner Gitt started his career at the German Federal Institute of Physics and Technology (Physikalisch-Technische Bundesanstalt 'PTB'), Brunswick, as Head of Data Processing. In 1978 he was promoted to Director and Professor at the PTB. He has written numerous scientific papers in the field of information science, as well as many others concerned with mathematics an control engineering. Besides his scientific publications he is well known as author of several popular books, some of which have been translated into Bulgarian, Czech, English, Finnish, French, Hungarian, Italian, Polish, Russian. Since 1980 he has been a member of the executive board of the Study Group 'Word and Knowledge'. In 1966 Werner Gitt married his wife Marion. They have two children, Carsten and Rona.

1st English Edition 1995
2nd English Edition 2001

© of the German edition:
Werner Gitt, "Und die anderen Religionen"
1991 by CLV · Christliche Literatur-Verbreitung
Postfach 11 01 35 · D-33661 Bielefeld

© of the English Edition
1994 by CLV · Christliche Literatur-Verbreitung
Postfach 11 01 35 · D-33661 Bielefeld
Distribution for South Africa:
R. Steinberg, c/o SIM SA
P.O. Box 129, Mondeor 2110 RSA

Translation to English: Dr. Royal Truman
Correction: Lisa Woll-Schaaf
Cover: Dieter Otten, Bergneustadt
Typography: Enns Schrift & Bild, Bielefeld
Printed in Germany: by Ebner Ulm

ISBN 3-89397-765-1

# Table of Contents

# Foreword

We live in a time in which one can travel to nearly all places of the world. We constantly come into contact with other people, cultures, life-styles and also other *religions*. In addition, modern mass media provides us with much more information than was available in former times. In view of the many religious systems, the old question is posed anew, whether each can be saved in his own manner, or whether in the final analysis, there is only one way to God. In many places this is discussed passionately. Since we are obviously dealing with a very basic question, which involves our eternal destiny, it is worthwhile to intensely pursue an answer to this burning question. This will be attempted in this book, "What About the Other Religions?". The title chosen for this book insinuates first of all, that Christianity is merely one of many other religions. If it should turn out to be the only correct one, which function and effects do the other religions have? A list of key questions arises: How should our relationship with the other systems be seen? What is our own position in the so-called Western Christian World? Have we ourselves experienced salvation or are we still searching? We will devote our attention to these questions.

For practical reasons, among others, we will use definitions from the Bible to show how biblical teachings about faith and life-style can be distinguished from other religious doctrines.

*Audience*: Based on the statement "Religion is a fundamental need of every person" (see chapter 4.2) and the central questions regarding religions which move all of us, this book is directed toward everyone: to those who have founded their lives firmly on Biblical faith, as well as to those who are still seeking. We invite Christians and members of other religions, even if for differing reasons, to read, to inform themselves and to act. The book is directed furthermore to young and old, to intellectuals and those who do not feel they belong to this category. It is directed to the reader without any Bible knowledge as well as to those who already know the Bible well. That sounds so all-encompassing, as though everyone is really meant; there is, however, a restriction: if you are absolutely convinced about the righteousness of your life-style up to now and do not wish to change your behaviour in any way, then you should not read this book. You will only upset yourself, and we would like to spare you the annoyance.

*Method*: The phrase "One must see the complicated things in simple terms, if one wishes to go into depth" came from the German Federal Chancellor *Konrad Adenauer* (1876-1967). In this sense, *one* central idea guides us through this book: the path is clearly marked by the perhaps unexpected word "invention". If this idea is kept in mind throughout the whole book, then the reader will eventually find himself at the goal.

Most of the citations from the Bible are given as direct quotations from the *New International Version* (first published in Great Britain 1979), so that the reader will not have to pause and refer to the Bible. References to literature or quotes are given in square brackets (for example, [K3,11]). They consist of an abbreviation which uses the first letter of the book, author's name (or editor) followed by a sequential number. If another number follows, it represents the page number of the source mentioned.

*Thanks*: Once again, I am thankful to my loving wife for having taken over the secretarial duties. CLV (Christliche Literatur-Verbreitung) publisher's readers have given me their constructive criticism of the manuscript, which I have gladly taken into account.

It is our prayer that this paperback will be a help to many readers with questions about the faith. Our ultimate goal would be accomplished, if searching people find the living faith and say, "We have found the one Moses wrote about in the Law, and about whom the prophets, also wrote – Jesus" (John 1:45).

# Preface to the English Edition

As author I am delighted that, after translations into Russian, Hungarian and Czech, my book is now available in English. *Dr Royal Truman* was responsible for the arduous task of translating the book into his mother tongue. His German wife *Petra* was a great help to him. Mrs. *Sarah Jayne Curtius* later translated the additional chapter 9.2 on sects. Mrs. *Lisa Woll-Schaaf* proof read the translation thoroughly. I would like to thank all of those involved for their work in making this book come about. May it be a help to those who are seeking and asking questions as well as to those who already believe.

*Werner Gitt*

# 1 Introduction

This book deals thoroughly with an emotional issue which is discussed among both Christians and non-Christians. This issue can be outlined in four questions which are often posed:

- All men are searching for truth. Should we not examine all religions, since surely each contains at least some partial truth?

- There are so many religions. Are all wrong, is there a true one, or do all lead in the end to the same goal?

- Many people lived before Jesus came into this world, and before the Christian message was announced. Where will those who lived then spend eternity?

- There are so many people, who have had no opportunity to hear the Gospel. Will they nevertheless be saved, or are they all lost?

From numerous discussions, the author knows that these questions belong to the most frequently asked during conversations about the Christian faith. Many pose the above questions after having heard the Gospel in order to avoid having to make a personal commitment. Usually, however, these are honest questions for which a clear Biblical answer is being sought.

We wish, therefore, to deal with these "hot potatoes" and will do so with the following assumptions:

- A binding answer can only be provided by God himself. We would like to present the Biblical statements whether they agree with our personal tastes or not. In order to understand God's Word, one must think carefully.

- The *whole* Bible is *God's inspired word* (2 Tim 3:16) and carries the seal of truth (John 17:17). If we hold on steadfast, we will stand on a solid rock foundation instead of sinking in the quicksand of human speculation.

In this book we consider the phenomenon of the multitude of religions from the perspective of man's creative nature. Where man finds a gap, he invents something. He creates something. He fills the "hole" with either intellectual or material matter. Most people trust in inventions to solve problems. In this modern age, faith in technology has often replaced religions faith. But even religions are man-made inventions, as we will show, born from human creativity, to fill gaps where knowledge of the Creator and His character are missing. With this in mind, we can most easily deal with the theme of this book by using the key word "inventions". In so doing, we shall distinguish between **four kinds of inventions**.

If we constantly keep in mind the two questions:

- **Who** made each specific invention?
- **Why** was this invention made?

we will systematically find a solution to the problem we have set out to understand.

# 2 Applied Human Creativity: Millions of Patents

Man has the gift of creativity, and his inventiveness is simply immeasurable. Whenever man has a problem, he gives intensive thought to it and searches for a solution. The statistics from the German Patent Office (DPA = Deutsches Patentamt) in Munich may help us to establish a tangible, lasting impression of the extent of man's creative activities [D1]. Between the years 1948 and 1989, a huge number of patents, 2,426,739, was registered at the DPA. The German contribution amounted to 1,552,333 patents. In Munich, during 1989, 41,244 were filed. The German Patent Office in Munich is one of the largest technical libraries in the world. It includes 800,000 volumes and contains 16.5 million patent documents from Germany and abroad. Let us consider briefly some reports:

**Agriculture:** Human inventions include such spectacular things as the aeroplane, the computer and the telephone, which have changed our lives considerably, as well as principles and methods which are useful for daily life. Many inventions had precursors, which, when new, raised consderable attention, but today merely have value as museum pieces. In this respect, the modern history of agriculture would be incomplete without considering the development of steam plows. *Figure 1* shows a very special type of plough, the steam spade plough [H2], built in the year 1877. This several-ton heavy monster was driven by a steam engine and was unique, because through its new technology, the plough could be used to turn over the earth, and at the same time, crumble and mix it. As man's creative spirit has been repeatedly applied to solving agricultural problems, tractor-driven multi-purpose plows have long ago replaced steam ploughs.

**Medicine:** If we consider the technical status of medicine, we recognise that it was fundamentally changed through the inven-

# Der Dampf-spatenpflug

Darbys Pedestrian-Breitgrabema-
schine von 1877. Österreichisches
Landwirthschaftliches Wochen-
blatt, 5 (1879) S. 61.

**Figure 1:** *The Steam Spade Plough from the year 1877. Derby's Pedestrian Wide-Digging Machine from 1877 (Austrian Agrarian Weekly, 5 (1879), p. 61)*

tion of the microscope. *Louis Pasteur* (1822-1895) came to the conclusion, only last century, that certain microorganisms are the cause of illnesses. Only a hundred years ago *Robert Koch* (1843-1910) discovered the tuberculosis bacillus and the cholera virus, and thus led the victory over terrible epidemics.

Another major breakthrough using new technical methods to diagnose disease came in 1895 when *Wilhelm Conrad Röntgen* (1845-1923) discovered X-rays. It became possible for the first time to make internal parts of the body visible without surgical means. One scientist recently determined: "Through the discovery of X-rays, more human lives have been saved than those lost through all wars to date". With the recent discovery of fiber optics, internal body cavities (such as the stomach and bowel) can be observed directly and diseased parts diagnosed. Today application of computer tomography even allows soft parts of the body to be shown in three dimensions without using damaging X-rays. 20th century medicine has made improvements in heath care possible which suffering people of earlier centuries could only dream of. A few examples from a wide spectrum illustrate this: new diagnostic methods; new types of medicines from sulfamides to antibiotics; new operational techniques, such as microsurgery, transplantation of organs, coagulation by means of light rays, and surgery with laser beams. Since the first heart transplant in 1968, over 10,000 hearts have been transplanted world-wide. The one-year survival rate of 64 % in 1980 increased to almost 90 % by 1989.

**Computers:** The computer is, beyond doubt, one of the most spectacular discoveries of our century. Today high-performance computers manage several billion computing operations per second, and micro-computers become ever faster, easier to use, cheaper and smaller. Computers have found applications in all areas of research, the economy, and increasingly, in everyday life.

The German inventor *Konrad Zuse* (born in 1910) is considered the pioneer of the programmable computer. In **1936** he built the Z1. That was a strictly mechanical computer with a tact frequency of 0.2 Hertz. The Z1 was destroyed during the war, but the construction documents still exist today. In 1983 *Zuse* began the reconstruction of the Z1 with the help of Siemens AG, Bad Hersfeld, Germany. Today the functional replica (*Figure 2*) comprises the key feature of the computer exhibition in the *Museum of Communications and Technology* (Museum für Verkehr und Technik) in Berlin. By **1941**, *Zuse* finished building the Z3, the first electrical computing machine, consisting of 2400 relays. A mutiplication took 4 to 5 seconds at that time. A further advancement was the use of electron tubes. The American ENIAC computer was functional by **1946,** with 17,000 electron tubes and other components. The machine weighed 30 metric tons, and managed a multiplication in 2.8 thousandths of a second. The second generation of computers appeared in **1955** with significantly smaller transistors. Inte-

**Figure 2.** *The German inventor, Konrad Zuse, and his assistants Schweier and Saupe, during the reconstruction of the world's first computer.*

grated switching, a new technology which allowed the building of switching and other components out of the same material, was introduced in **1958**. The constant increase in the number of switching elements on each silicon chip led the way to the third generation computers.

During recent years, the number of switching functions per chip has doubled almost every two years. We are now able to store all the telephone numbers of a good-sized city on a single chip. *Figure 3* shows a 16-megabit chip as it was first developed in **1990**. *Microcomputers* deliver a better performance today than huge mainframe computers did 20 years ago, and no limits on how much further the size can be decreased and the speed increased are foreseeable. *Supercomputers* perform today at breath-taking speed. The fastest computer executes over 10 billion computer operations per second, and this record will soon be surpassed.

**Figure 3.** *The 16-Megabit Chip: 700 Typewritten Pages on a Fingertip (Siemens Press).*

*Only with a magnifying glass can the police recognise and analyse fingerprints, which are different for every person. The fine-structure of a comparably-sized microchip, however, can only be made out through a microscope. Almost 34 million building elements have been integrated on this 16 million-bit chip, integrated by Siemens. 240,000 tiny switching and storage components must be placed on the surface of a square millimetre. The smallest elements measure only slightly more than a half thousandths of a millimetre. For comparison: a human hair is 100 times thicker. This electronic building block consists of one of the newest generation of dynamic storage. It can store 16 million (more exactly: 16·1024·1024 = 16,777,216) information units (bits). That corresponds to a text size of 700 typewritten pages. This book, therefore, could be stored seven times over on an area the size of a fingertip.*

**Unusual Inventions:** Human creativity has brought forth products which now make up a collection of oddities causing us to grin. Thus, in 1910 patent number 235,849 was registered with the German Patent Office (DRP 235 849; Deutsches Reichspatent) as "Protection against theft and exchange of headware". It was explained that: "The invention works as follows: In the secured position, the device blocks the cavity of the headware by using a blocking element which extends across the cavity, thus making use of the headware impossible and perhaps enabling the headware to be locked onto a hat stand."

Numerous inventors found the speed of walking insufficient and sought to solve this problem. *Robert Michael* from Leipzig registered (DRP 152 505) in 1903 his "*Curved Shoes*", a device to increase the length of one's step (*Figure 4*). In the patent application, one reads: "The curved shoe should allow quick forward movement of people and, if need be, permit the walker to go over obstacles, without removing the gadget". Eventually it occurred to *Georg Erich Haehnel* from Griesheim, Germany, in 1920, to attach gas motor cylinders under the feet, to allow forward jumps to be made (DRP 353 119). Another curious collection of inventions promises to increase the enjoyment of bathing. *Figure 5* is a self-explanatory illustration of patent number DRP 51 766 applied for by *Carl Dittmann* in 1889, a "*Wave Bath Rocker*."

An invention which is now hard to comprehend was based on ideas from *Daniel Keutmann* and *August Coutelle* from Essen, Germany. Patent DRP 142 380 was granted in 1902 for a device for parting hair. The patent was worded as follows: "With it every man will be in the position to part his hair quickly, anywhere, without help from others, that is, to make an exact part, which falls in two exact portions in a line on both sides of the head."

**Perpetual Motion Machines:** Another group of inventions which cannot be ignored are "perpetual motion devices". Inventors with this goal often invested their whole lives and

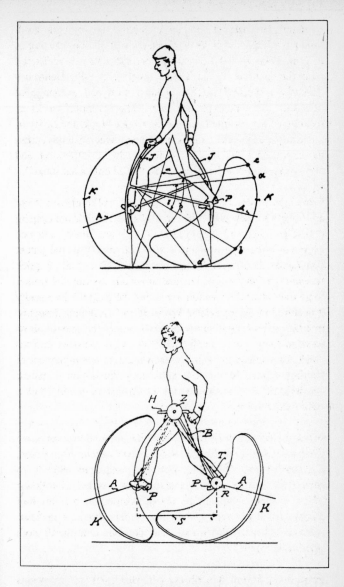

**Figure 4:** *Curved shoes from Robert Michael (1903), a device to increase the length of one's stride (DRP 152 505).*

**Figure 5:** *Wave-bath swing by Carl Dittmann (1889), a device to increase the enjoyment of bathing (DRP 51 766).*

material possessions attempting to invent a utopian machine which runs forever, without the need to pump in energy. Had they been aware of and believed in fundamental laws of nature (for example, the First and Second Laws of Thermodynamics), which preclude the creation of these kinds of devices, they would have saved themselves a great deal of trouble. Even today some inventors concern themselves with questions which in reality amount to no more than a search for perpetual motion devices. The machine from *Alessandro Capra,* shown in *Figure 7,* is supposed to illustrate a wheel, which once set in motion, will run forever, without the need for additional energy. The impossibility of this type of *perpetual motion* is explained by the physical law of conservation of energy which states that energy cannot be created or destroyed. The perpetual motion researchers have nevertheless done science a significant service: through their tireless efforts, they have demonstrated that laws of nature cannot be outwitted by human cleverness.

**Types of Inventions:** When one considers the usefulness of various inventions, one can make the following classifications:

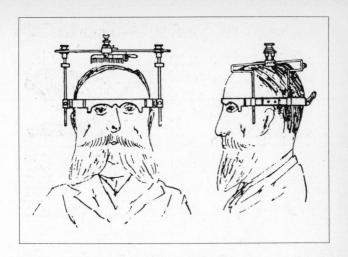

**Figure 6:** *Device to part the hair on a man's head by Daniel Keutmann and August Coutelle (1902: DRP 142 380).*

**1.** There are numerous technical inventions, which have made our lives much easier and improved human existence: pens, telephones, cars and electric lights belong to items we take for granted in our daily lives. Human inventiveness was effective in their creation. Modern medical equipment and methods, without which our hospitals would not be thinkable, ranging from adhesive bandages to heart-lung machines, also belong to this category.

**2.** There are inventions which never attained any meaning and now belong to a group of antique oddities [L1].

**3.** There are inventive attempts to make the impossible possible. The ideas behind the perpetual motion machines are complex plans which can not be converted into real inventions. They are regrettable, but, with the recognition of the law of conservation of energy by *Julius Robert Meyer* (1814-1878), now avoidable mistakes.

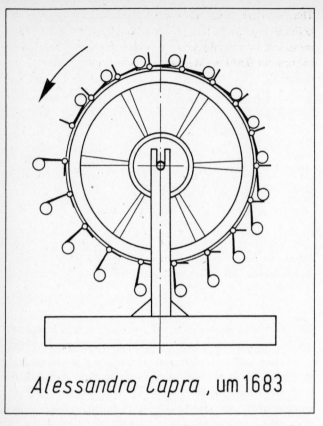

Alessandro Capra, um 1683

**Figure 7:** *Idea for a perpetual motion device by Alessandro Capra (1683).*

**4.** Finally, there are inventions which should never have been made, since they only lead to human troubles, misery, pain and death. To these belong all war tools as well as instruments and methods of torture.

The human gift of creativity is not limited to technical problems; it also includes all areas of life and human activities.

Thus, man has created all possible philosophies, ideologies and political systems. In fact, human creativity stops at nothing; it seeks solutions to all problems. In this chapter we have gotten to know the **first type of invention**. Man is the inventor.

# 3 What No Patent Office Has Recorded

Some particulary ingenious constructions and concepts cause us to marvel each time we see them. Yet we do not find them registered in any patent office. Here are a few examples:

- Did you know that a **woodpecker** can bang its head against a tree trunk with a speed of 25 km/h without getting a concussion? A well-padded brain was designed for him so that he does not even get a headache.

- Did you know that there are birds which can fly forwards, backwards, sideways and vertically, or simply remain in place? An artistic, all-purpose drive was invented for the **humming-bird**. With up to 80 wing flaps per second, he attains a frequency which surpasses the alternating current frequency used in Europe (50 Hz) by 60 %. Humming-birds breathe 250 times per minute, and their hearts beat over 1000 times during this period.

- Did you know that the **donkey-penguin's** body offers a flow resistance relative to its cross-sectional area (known as the drag coefficient $c_w$) which is better (lower) then that attained by all known flow coefficient optimised vehicles, whether submarine boot, race car or blimps. This penguin has such an ideal form, that it can perform elegant and fast swim manoeuvres with minimal energy expenditure.

- Did you know that there are **fish** which live at a depth of 10,000 meters underwater, in total darkness, and are equipped with lamps which convert energy with 100 % efficiency into light? Lamps of diverse colours which lose no energy in the form of heat loss were invented. (Lamps built by humans attain efficiencies in merely the 10 % range).

- Did you know that through **photosynthesis**, which occurs in every leaf, the energy in sunlight is converted into chemical energy? Did you know that no chemist or engineer has been able to duplicate this ingenious energy-conversion process?

- Did you know that the **human heart** beats 100,000 times per day and 2.5 milliard (= 2,500,000,000 !) times in 70 years? By that time a skyscraper could be filled with blood. All parts of the body are provided with blood through a densely branched 2500 km network of arteries, veins and capillaries – which is equivalent to the distance between Paris and Moscow. A maintenance-free pump was invented for this purpose which usually lasts a whole life long without the need for replacement parts.

- Did you know that the human genome (chromosomes) contains 3 milliard genetic letters? If someone wrote this chain of letters in a single row with a typewriter, it would reach from the North Pole to the Equator. A good secretary with a typing speed of 300 keystrokes per minute and 220 workdays per year, working 8 hours per day without interruption, could not type this huge number of letters during her whole working life. She would be busy with this task for 95 years! The storage medium, in the form of a double stranded spiral DNA molecule, requires a volume of only 3 milliardth of a cubic millimetre ($3 \cdot 10^{-9}$ mm$^3$). A huge storage density is achieved, manifold greater than can be attained by the most modern computers. To grasp the storage density of this material, we can imagine taking the material from the head of a pin with a diameter of 2 mm and stretching it out into a wire, which has the same diameter as a DNA molecule. How long would this wire be? Well, it would extend 33 times around the equator! Can you imagine that?

- Did you know that a trained programmer can write an average of 40 lines of programming code per day, taking into account the time from conception to system maintenance? In order to programme the number of characters in the **human genome**, it would be necessary to dedicate the entire working lives of an army of over 8000 programmers exclusively to this project. However, no human programmer knows how this programme, which fits on a stretched out DNA strand only 1 meter in length, should be arranged.

- Did you know that the storage medium, which appears in every living cell, represents the **highest known storage density**? If one calculates the amount of information contained in the human genome in terms of 160-page paperbacks, then it corresponds to almost 12,000 books. Recalling the astonishing amount of information which can be stored on a 16-megabit chip (*Figure 3*), we must be deeply impressed by the fact that the human DNA strands allow over 1400 times more information to be stored.

Thinking in terms of paperbacks, the amount of information in a spot of DNA the size of the head of a needle would fill 15 billion (= $15 \cdot 10^{12}$) books! Laid on top of each other, that is a stack 500 times higher than the distance between the earth and the moon, a good 384,000 km. Or if we were to distribute this pile of books among the inhabitants on earth (5 milliard people), each would receive 3000 copies!

If we consider the inventions of the type mentioned above, the purpose of their creation is easy to understand. If however we ask about the originator, the inventor, of all these concepts, then undoubtably no human being comes into consideration. Only a single really satisfying answer remains: they are the **work of the Creator**! (For more information, see [G1]).

This fundamental recognition of God's existence, arising from the conclusion that a creation requires a Creator, is available to every person, whether the message of the Bible has reached him or not. Someone once asked a Bedouin how he knew there was a God. He answered in this manner: "How do I know whether a person or camel walked by my tent at night? I see it from the tracks on the sand. Who is able to look around this

26

world without noticing God's tracks?" The Old Testament speaks about a way, available to all, in which one can recognise God's existence, by observing nature: "The heavens declare the glory of God ... There is no speech or language where their voice is not heard" (Ps 19:1-3). In this matter none has an excuse, since "They although knew God, they neither glorified him as God nor gave thanks to him ..." (Rom 1:21). All primitive tribes demonstrate their belief in a God with some manner of worship. The ancient heathen philosophers also confirm the truth of the above claim:

*Aristotle* (384-322 BC): "God, who is invisible to each mortal form of life, is visible through His works."

*Plato* (427-347 BC): "The world must have had an origin. This origin is the eternal Creator."

*Cicero* (106-43 BC): "The heavens and stars demonstrate clearly that they are controlled by a god-form which surpasses the wisdom of all human understanding."

In this chapter we have learned about the **second type of inventions.** Their inventor is God.

# 4 Human Religions: 1000 Different Paths

## 4.1 Man's Problem

Our greatest problem with the Creator, whose existence we are all aware of, is our guilt feelings towards God and our fellow men. Since the Fall of Man, man lives separated from God, and his bad conscience is evidence of his condition:

> "Indeed, when **Gentiles,** (= *people who do not know the God of the Bible*), who who do not have the law, do by nature things required by the law, they are a law, for themselves, even though they do not have the law, since they show that the requirements of the law are written on their hearts, their consciences also bearing witness, and their thoughts now accusing, now even defending them." (Rom 2:14-15).

In the *Good News* (1982) these important verses are translated as follows, and are easier to understand:

> "The other people do not have God's Law. But there are among them people who through natural feeling do what the Law requires. Although not explained to them, they carry this understanding in themselves. Their behaviour shows that the demands of the Law are written in their hearts, and this is proven by their consciences, whose voice alternately accuses or defends them."

By giving man a conscience, the creator has provided not only born-again believers but also heathens with an indicator which demonstrates that there is good and evil. The Greek word for conscience in the New Testament is "syneidesis" and means "accessory". It is a court, which experiences everything a person does and thinks. God in His creative work has ennobled us with this component of His likeness. God has in this way, as well as in many others, clearly distinguished us from animals, who cannot judge their own actions on moral grounds. Man knows, however, that he must someday answer for his actions. Wrong behaviour, called "sin" in the Bible, burdens us and thus demonstrates the gap between man and God. This situation has been recognised throughout time as a fundamental problem, and thus human creativity became active in an attempt to:

- make things right with God and
- make peace with our conscience.

Man has made many attempts to reach this goal. Many different concepts of God have been created. These are expressed in thousands of religions. A few examples are briefly described here:

**Polytheism** (Greek: *polys* = many; *many gods*): Several or many gods are worshipped.

**Monotheism** (Greek: *monos* = single, one; *doctrine of one god*): This is based on the concept that a single god exists as the highest being. (For a more exact differentiation, one must distinguish between monotheism and trinity monotheism [S4]). Believers in evolution view monotheism as the highest level of religious development.

**Pantheism** (Greek: *pan* = all, entire; *doctrine of god in everything*): God is seen in the universe and in nature. In other words, god and nature are one and the same. The German philosopher *Schopenhauer* called pantheism the finest form of atheism.

**Theism** (Greek: *theos* = god; *belief in god*): According to this doctrine, there is a single, personal god, outside and beyond the world, that keeps everything running and rules over all, but does not demand any specific behaviour from man, and seeks no relationship with him.

**Deism** (Latin: *deus* = god; *doctrine of a god*): This doctrine, which was developed in England, during the age of enlightenment, assumes that a god set the gears of the universe into motion, but no longer has anything more to do with it. Well-known adherents were *Voltaire*, *Rousseau* and *Lessing*.

**Atheism** (Greek: *atheos* = without god, *godless*): This is a philosophy of life (and therefore a form of religion) which does not recognise any form of god. In the study of religions, one distinguishes between theistical and atheistical religions (for example, the Hinayana-Buddhism and the older Taoism). In the "Christian" countries, atheism is often understood as a movement against Christianity: "There is no after-life, no reunion". The Marxist, *August Bebel*, noted that, "If there is actually a God, then we are the real idiots."

**New Age**: This is an attempt to combine far-eastern religiousness with modern ideas of progressive evolution. The New-Age movement promises to resolve all current crises due to conflicting interests through the rise of a higher unit which combines nature, man and God in a new paradise.

**Syncretism** (late greek: *syncretismus* = federation of Cretan cities): The fusion of different religions, world views and philosophical doctrines to form a new doctrine. (Unification of parties instead of fighting between them.)

According to *primitive religions*, powers and beings which Man tries to please through sacrifices and rituals or ward off through magical incantations live in nature. These concepts are called:

**Animism** (Latin: *anima* = soul; *belief in soul*): Everything in nature is believed to have a soul. Animism is expressed as the belief that nature is full of innumerable spirits, including those of ancestors and ghosts, but it also appears, in monotheistic religions.

**Fetishism** (Portuguese: *Magical means*): Lifeless objects are honoured and prayed to, since they are supposed to possess secret powers. The belief by modern Man in amulets and talisman is included in this category.

**Totemism** (Indian): This is the belief that a tribe or individual has descended from an object in nature. Accordingly, a group of people supposedly arises either from an animal, a plant, a stone or some other object, and is related to the object. The *totem* is an embodiment of a powerful protector of the tribe and is worshipped as a symbol of closeness of man with nature.

## 4.2 What Is a Religion?

Before repeatedly using the term religion, we must define exactly what we mean by it. This is necessary, since there are many definitions of religion. The numerous terms used for the phenomenon we call religion reflect the various aspects of this concept [B3, 5]: The Latin word *religio* used by the Romans was understood by *Cicero* as cautious respect towards something important, as a conscientious feeling of duty towards the gods. In Greek, the term *eusebeia* (fear towards God, piety) played a similar role. The Arabic and new Persian word *din* emphasises the legal aspects. The Indian word *dharma* (Sanskrit) or *dhamma* (Pali) means, "that which man should abide by", meaning the law. On the other hand, the Chinese *chiao*, Japanese *kyo* and Korean *hak* refer to "The Doctrine."

**Definitions of religion according to modern religious studies:**
In his book, "Marxism – Opium for the People?" [S2] *Thomas Schirrmacher* dealt with various definitions of religion, as developed by religious scholars. This study produced no unique and binding statement; rather, the religious investigator, *Christoph Elsas*, has collected and organised hundreds of definitions. In the comparative study of religions, no religion can be chosen to serve as a standard example with which other types of religions can be compared. The religious spectrum is so broad, that only a few common characteristics can be found. Four definitions are mentioned here from the many available [S2, 46-47]:

(1) "The specific function of religion lies in providing fundamental concepts, which convert the uncertain and unknow-
able into certain and comprehensible" *(Niklas Luhmann)*.

(2) "A religious system describes a framework of conceptual
elements (and the related actions, representations and
objects) which fulfil the function of providing man with an
explanation of his world, which is not further reducible,
and with norms for his behaviour, which cannot be further
simplified" (*Ulrich Berner*).

(3) "Every religion reduces life and the world's history to the
central questions. These are the norms and values which
can merely be accepted, but not proved, and which comprise the substance of religion" *(Thomas Schirrmacher)*.

(4) Religion is a manner of human existence arising from the
relationship between sense and reason, in which the reason
allowing for the sense in the different religions is understood either extra-worldly or intra-worldly (*H. R. Schlette,
G. J. Bellinger [B3, 5]*).

From these broad statements, which go well-beyond the concepts mentioned in section 4.1, a fundamental sentence can be
derived:

**Religion is a fundamental need of every man!**

Similarly, the Russian religious critic *Nikolai Berdjajew* concluded: "Man is incurably religious." The assumption of a higher
being or the practice of prayers and rituals, according to definitions (1) to (4), is not a prerequisite for a religion. Its existence,
however, is sufficient to characterise a system as a religion.

Every man needs an explanation for the world in which he
lives, and he needs norms to direct his actions. This is the
starting point of a religion [B3, 5]: "Religion begins the moment people with a particular philosophy of life come to the
conclusion, that those values and goals which they find sensible

can be used to describe standards for living." In this sense, not only is Christianity a religion, but Marxism is also a special form of religion. The Marxist also believes in fundamental principles, such as that matter is eternal, that man was created to work, and that the dialectic principles of history will ultimately bring about a communist society. National socialism proclaimed similar basic convictions, so that this also constitutes a religion [S3]. *Hitler* always spoke of "Providence" as a higher being. We easily recognise a form of prayer when we consider the "confession of faith" to *Hitler* written by the Nazi youth leader *Baldur von Schirach* [R2, 42]:

"We often heard the sound of your voice,
and listened quietly and folded our hands,
since every word penetrated our soul.
We all know it: the end will come,
which will free us from danger and trouble.
What is a year in the passing of time!
What sort of law is there, which can hinder,
the pure belief which you have given us,
which determines our young lives.
My Leader, only you are my path and goal!"

Art can also play the role of a religion. *Richard Wagner* (1813-1883) wrote the following "confession of faith", which from its outward appearance seems Christian-like, but its content has nothing at all to do with Christianity [W1, 62-63]:

"I believe in God, *Mozart* and *Beethoven,* and on their disciples and apostles;
I believe in the Holy Spirit and in the truth of a single, indivisible art;
I believe this art comes from God and lives in the hearts of all enlightened men;
I believe that once one indulges in the exalted pleasures of this higher art, one must surrender oneself to it forever and can never deny it;
I believe that through this art all can be saved, and everyone is allowed to famish to death for it;

33

I believe that I will be highly blessed through death;

I believe I was a dissonant chord on earth, but upon death will be made glorious and redeemed.

I believe in a Final Judgment which will dreadfully punish all those in this world who dared to profiteer from this pure art, who disgraced and dishonoured it out of an evil heart and vile greed for sensation;

I believe they will be sentenced to hear their own music forever;

I believe, however, that the true disciples of this high art will become transfigured in a heavenly web of divine sounds and united forever with the godly spring of harmony.

May this be my happy destiny! Amen."

**A Definition of religion derived from the Bible:** In the following considerations, we will not refer to one of the many definitions from the comparative study of religions, but to one derived from the Bible. We do this because we do not wish to look at religion subjectively (see Chapter 5.3). The word "religion" doesn't appear directly in the Bible, but the topic is precisely described. An important statement in this respect appears in Psalms 96:5:

> "All gods of the people are idols,
> but the Lord has made the heavens."

Considering additional statements from the Bible, we define religion as follows:

---

**Definition of religion (derived from the Bible) (D1):**

A religion is

- any and every human concept of God, as well as
- every philosophy with undisputable statements of belief and norms for behaviour,

which consciously or unconsciously replaces the Creator God mentioned in the Bible.

---

According to our definition **D1**, which gives rise to all the following considerations, the belief in the God of the Bible and in Jesus Christ cannot in any way be confused with religion. It is noteworthy that Christianity has been represented throughout history as a religion. Thus, *Luther's* 95 theses were an appeal to turn away from the practices of a church, a religion, and towards the Gospel. Even some "Christian" sects follow more and more the path of religion.

Which systems do we count among religions? The following three-fold organisation should make the analysis easier:

**1. Religions in a narrow sense:** Systems which we can denote as religions according to popular opinion, since gods or spirits, priests, and temples are officially involved. Prayers and rituals play an important role (for example, Islam, Hinduism).

**2. Philosophical systems** in which, in general, no gods are worshipped, but which clearly replace the position of the Biblical Creator (for example, Marxism, National Socialism, Anthroposophy): The theory of evolution, according to definition **D1**, is also clearly a religion, since the Creator is not viewed as the cause of life, but another explanation is offered instead. Thus, the biologist *Sir Julian Huxley* [U1] writes:

> "For me personally, the rejection of the idea of God as a supernatural being is an enormous spiritual relief... Darwinism removed the idea of a Creator-God from the sphere of rational statements."

Along these lines, based on numerous quotes from adherents of the theory of evolution, *Eduard Ostermann* has formulated these views as a religious belief [O2, 50-51]. In the theory of evolution, mutations, selection, randomness, the need for survival, and unlimited time are the gods which replace the person of a Creator. Jeremiah 10:11 refers to such gods: "These gods, who did not make the heavens and the earth, will perish from the earth and from under the heavens."

**3. Inconspicuous Religions**, which at first do not appear to be religions, but rather individual philosophies about life: To these belong, for example, what Jesus mentioned as Mammon. Mammon is a term from the Aramaic language, which means wealth and luxury.

In Luke 16:13, Jesus said: "You cannot serve both God and Money". Money represents here an alternative to God. The love of money and materialism replace the belief in the God of the Bible. Therefore, this is clearly another religion according to our previous definition **D1**. In other words, religion is everything which competes with the Biblical beliefs: What can I rely on completely? What gives my life meaning? Where does my heart lie? From where do I derive the fundamental decisions of my life? What do I love above all else? On what do I orient my actions? Jesus said, "For where your treasure is, there your heart will be also" (Matt 6:21).

The religion of Mammon was already mentioned in the Old Testament: Job posed the relevant questions:

> "If I have put my trust in gold or said to pure gold, 'You are my security', if I have rejoiced over my great wealth, the fortune my hands had gained" (Job 31:24-25).

He also recognised Mammon as a substitute for the living God, when he reached the logical conclusion: "This also would be sins to be judged, for I would have been unfaithful to God on high" (Job 31:28).

## 4.3 The Origins of Religions

No culture or civilisation has been found in which some form of religion does not exist. The question arises, "Where does religion come from?" To shed light on its origins, we distinguish between two points of view:

**1. The evolutionary point of view:** According to this view, the origins of religions (as well as life) are to be understood as a process of development, in which a simple polytheism arose after the belief in spirits and other powers and, over the course time developed into monotheism (Judaism, Christianity, Islam). The idea that religions originate through a process of development is derived from evolutionary concepts, in which evolution is taken to be a universally valid concept. This underlying assumption cannot, however, be grounded on historical facts, since polytheistic religions do not appear only in primitive cultures, but in the history of many groups of people, independent of the current cultural development, and often polytheistic and monotheistic forms of worship alternated over time (example: Egypt and Niniveh).

**2. The Biblical point of view:** According to the Bible, all men have been given three fundamental pieces of evidence (See *Figure 8*):

- The works of creation allow us to conclude there is a Creator (Rom 1:19-21).
- Our consciences convince us that we are guilty in God's eyes (Rom 2:14-15).
- A sense of eternity has been placed by God in our hearts (Eccl 3:11).

This general knowledge has greatly stimulated man's creative nature and led to thousands of forms of religion. By the time of *Cain and Able,* the difference between human and God's religious ways was already clear. *Cain* was the first person who wished to worship God in his own manner; he can, therefore be considered the founder of the first religion. *Cain* did not in any way preach polytheism, as supposed by an evolutionary viewpoint. His brother acted according to God's will and was, therefore, mentioned as an example of a God-pleasing believer (Hebr 11:4). Thus our chain of faith goes back from *Abraham, Noah and Enoch* to the first people. This demonstrates that from the very beginning, faith which pleases God was always there, and parallel to it, religions arose as human ideas. Thus,

| The Three Non-Biblical Sources of Information | Heathen Evidence (Source: Man) | Biblical Statements (Source: God) |
|---|---|---|
| Creation 1 → God's Existence | Aristotle: "God who is invisible to all mortal beings, is visible through his works." Cicero: "The heavens and stars show clearly that they are guided by a god." | Rom 1:19: "Since what may be known about God is plain to them." Ps 19:1-3: "The heavens declare the glory of God; ... There is no speech or language where there voice is not heard." |
| Con-science 2 → Existence of God's Law | The many human religions | Rom 2:15: "Since they show that the requirements of the law are written in their hearts, their consciences also bearing witness, and their thoughts now accusing, now even defending them." |
| Heart 3 → Existence of Eternity | Indians: Happy Hunting Ground. Greeks: Island of the Blessed. Moslems: Life of Luxury. Babylonians: Land of the Silver Heaven. | Eccl 3:11: "He has made everything beautiful in its time. He has also set eternity in the hearts of men." |

**Figure 8:** *Three Sources of Information, Available to Every Person: the Creation, Conscience, and Heart.*

monotheism is not the result of an evolutionary process. Though *Cain* still had the God of the Bible in mind with his sacrifice, nevertheless, he did not attain God's mercy (Gen 4:5).

According to Hebrews 11:4 he lacked faith, in contrast to *Abel*. In this matter, we can distinguish between two ways in which religions originated:

**2A. Collective Origin:** After the Flood, the human race, which descended from *Noah's* family, multiplied greatly and spread out over the whole earth (see the genealogical lines in Genesis 10). Through decadence, sociocultural decline and collective weakening of the original relationship with God, along with man's own contributions and inventiveness, each group of people, which arose through physical isolation, developed its own form of religion (*folk religions and tribal religions*). The Old Testament gives an eloquent impression of the numerous heathen religions and their characteristics. The Canaanites (and not only they) had such an abominable religion, that they burned their own children as sacrifices to serve their gods (Deut 12:31).

**2B. Origin through a religious founder:** Other religions have their source in a single founder, as for example Islam or Buddhism, who included elements of their own religious upbringing in their new teachings. But even Christian sects, with a wide spectrum of confusion and distortion of Biblical truths, can be often traced back to a single founder (*Founder religions*).

The *primitive religions* (tribal religions) have no known founder, no basic book, and thus no fixed doctrine in writing. The religious life centres around the medicine man, magician, shaman or priest and concepts passed on by word of mouth, partially as secret knowledge. In the folk religions (tribal religions), it is accepted that other tribes honour other gods and practice other religions. On the other hand, founder religions claim a general validity for all people.

## 4.4 Characteristics of Religions

At all times and in all parts of this earth, man has applied his creativeness to develop religions. The result is that there is a

39

multitude of religions instead of a single one. Up to now, we have assigned the origins of religions primarily to human creativeness. Another aspect must be considered: in this fallen world, the activities of the devil must not be underestimated, since his primary activity is to lie to man and lead him astray. Thus, the lies "Did God really say" (Gen 3:1) and "You will be like God" (Gen 3:5) led to the sinful fall of man. Satan spends a lot of effort trying to influence man to follow religious paths which do not lead to God, but to eternal damnation.

One thousand, the number of religions mentioned in the chapter title, can be viewed as much too low an estimate. Therefore, the question arises: Among all these different religions, is there at least a single correct one, or are all of them false? We will pursue this question later.

We wish now to consider the main characteristics of a religion. The well-known evangelist, *Wilhelm Pahls*, has named three characteristics which define most religions [P3]:

Religions deal with:

- people
- man-made rules
- objects

We now wish to examine these individual characteristics:

**1. The Human Factor:** The founder of a religion, as well as its prominent representatives, enjoy much recognition and authority. They are honoured in many ways: by pictures, statues, and by the distribution of their writings through their disciples. That applies to *Mohammed* and *Buddha*, as well as *Joseph Smith*, the founder of the Mormon religion. In the tribal religions this leading role is played by medicine men and priests.

**2. Man-Made Rules:** An immense and varied number of rules, rites and ceremonies have been created by man to please God.

The sacrifice of children belongs to the religious practices of the fertility cults. Thus, according to rough estimates made by American archeologists, over 20,000 children were sacrificed to Baal in Carthage between 400 and 200 BC at Tophet. The *Pharisees* of Israel had invented many rules which bound and limited man's actions, they did not free nor protect him, as intended by the simple commandments of God at Sinai. Jesus reproached them with the words, "Thus you nullify the word of God by your tradition that you have handed down. And you do many things like that" (Mark 7:13). Others have imposed inhuman penance on sinners, which enslave and dishonour man. There are even religious practices which distort the Biblical intention: people are punished, for example, by having to repeat a certain number of times the *Lord's Prayer.* We must reject this as false, since the Bible describes prayer to the Father as worship, praise, requests or thanks-giving, never as a punishment or ritual.

**3. Religious Objects:** Man has erected such gigantic objects in the name of religion, that, even today, they belong to man's most spectacular efforts. At Kyoto and Nara (Japan) one gets an impression of tremendous human toil. In Nara (from 710 to 784 AD, the capital of Japan) one finds the *Todaiji Temple,* the *largest wooden building in the world*: 58 m long, 51 m wide and 49 m high *(Figure 9)*. The largest bronze statue in the world is found in this building (16.2 m high, cast from of 437 metric tons of bronze, 130 kg gold and 75 kg of mercury). It is the largest figure of Buddha ever casted *(Figure 10)*. In the *Horyuji Temple* in Kyoto one sees the *"Thousand-handed Statue"* , which is worshipped along with 1000 other statues of Buddha *(Figure 11)*.

There are 220,000 religious buildings in Japan (Shinto shrine, Buddhist temples), and about two million people are involved full-time in nothing else but religious activities. In Japan worship plays a major role in society and involves the majority of the population. In front of the many cult centres, one sees how people light incense sticks or candles and bow down before statues and other objects.

**Figure 9:** *The Largest Wooden Construction in the World: the Buddhist Todaiji Temple in Nara (Japan).*

In our Christian western world, objects also play an important role in religion. Thus, the conscience can be appeased by obtaining a supposed piece of the True Cross or travelling to places where the bones of important people lay. (Should one collect all the pieces of the True Cross, it would make up a real forest).

All religions (in the narrow sense) have indeed recognised the fundamental problem of the separation of man from God and seek a human answer. This answer is: **religion**! It is a way which arises from man himself. If a religion is fundamental to a specific group of people, the moral demands of this religion often develop into a cultural tradition. *Heinrich Kemner* (1903-1993), the well-known pastor, evangelist and founder of the spiritual armament centre *(Geistliches Rüstzentrum Krelingen)* said, "Religion and tradition have indeed a protective power (in an ethical sense), but no power to save (with respect to eternity)." The religious traditions are very different in different countries:

- The Japanese have a Buddhist and Shintoist tradition
- The Indians have a Hindu tradition
- The Moslems have an Islamic tradition
- animists have the tradition of their tribal religion
- in the Christian western world, we have a Christian tradition.

Indeed there is a Christian religion, which has alsodeveloped rituals and mechanisms to numb the conscience. For example, if one deliberately breaks God's commandments during the Carnival season and then goes to a church on Ash Wednesday to get an ash cross, one has indeed numbed hisguilty conscien-

**Figure 10:** *The Largest Bronze Statue in the World: the Figure of Buddha in the Todaiji Temple in Nara (Japan).*

**Figure 11:** *Partial View of the Sanjusangendo Temple in Kyoto (Japan), with 1000 Statues of Buddha.*

ce with religion (and a Christian one at that!). In God's eyes, that is a hypocritical action with a pious touch, but without a true change of heart.

## 4.5  Are Religions from God or from Man?

We wish to select here some religions as examples and describe their various practices.

**Japan:** In Japanese households, there is a house altar, in which the dead are honoured and prayed to. It is believed that on the day someone dies, the spirits of the dead come and remain in the home. To provide well for them, grains of rice are laid out, since things are not so pleasant for them in hell. Only on the day of a death can they return to earth. After the celebration, straw boats are placed in the ocean, and lit on fire. Then the spirits of the dead leave this world again and return to hell.

**India:** Of the approximately 600 million Indians, some 500 million are Hindus. In this religion, many gods, spirits and demons are worshipped. The Hindus believe in reincarnation, that is, in the next life: one returns to earth in another form. Whoever has not proved himself in this life, returns to the world in the next life as a spider, fly, toad, rat or cow. A missionary, who worked in India, told me about poor people with small children who try to sleep at night on traffic islands in the large cities. Why do these people seek out such an inhospitable place? Do they like the traffic noise and exhaust fumes? Of course not! On the traffic islands there are no rats. If they slept in other places, they would be bitten as they slept by rats. In India there are 8 times as many rats as people. These gluttonous animals cannot be killed, however, since they could be the reincarnation of a person. To satisfy their hunger, these rats often attack small children and chew on their limbs as they sleep. It is abominable what religion makes possible. The largest cattle herd of a country is not found in the Pampas of Argentina, but in India which holds the world record with 30 million cows. Cows, which could be used for feeding people in this overpopulated land where many die of starvation, cannot be slaughtered on religious grounds.

**North Cameroon:** To calm the evil spirits, small children are "watered" with scalding water. The children are held tight, and hot water is poured down their mouths and throats. This torture ends with painful scalding and not seldom with the death of the child.

These few examples already demonstrate the horrible aspects of many religions, and one asks the question whether such rules could come from God. Well, these ideas could never come from the God of the Bible, the father of Jesus Christ, "The Lord is full of compassion and mercy" (James 5:11) and "God is love" (1 John 4:16).

Likewise, after close analysis, we conclude that all other religions (according to our definition **D1**; see Chapter 4.2) cannot have come from God. So we state:

**All religions are inventions of man!**

Four **types of inventions** were mentioned in the introduction; we have already discussed the first **three**. Two types are clearly of human origin (technical inventions and the religions) and the other obviously from a Godly source (works of creation). In the following chapters we go into detail about **the fourth type** of invention: **the Gospel!**

# 5 The Path from God to Man: the Gospel

The **Gospel** (Greek: *euaggélion* = happy message, good news; the saving message of Christ, the happy message from Jesus Christ) is the gift from God which makes salvation possible through Jesus Christ. Religion, on the other hand, is a human invention. The latter is, therefore, only an apparent solution. The human way leads astray, God's way, to the Father's house. God loves us and wishes to save us according to his plan. The Gospel is in this sense an invention. The inventor is not a human being, but God himself. We have up to this point learned about **four categories of inventions**, shown once again in *Figure 12*.

The meaning and the consequences of the Gospel, as well as its uniqueness and assumptions, will now be examined in detail. A necessary prerequisite to understanding these topics is that we listen to God's diagnosis of the human condition.

## 5.1 God's Diagnosis: God's Assessment of the Human Condition

We usually prefer to have a good opinion of ourselves, and poets often help us in this matter. *Goethe* wrote, "Noble is man, helpful and good." The world view of humanism, developed by *Lessing*, *Kant*, *Hegel* and others, is based on the assumption that man's essence is good. The French philosopher *Jean Jacques Rousseau* (1712-1778) influenced not only philosophical thinking; in fact, his view of the human being is seen even today as the basis of psychology, education and society. He coined the phrase, "Man is from nature good, and it follows, therefore, that he will remain so as long as no exterior influence ruins him." We see this view of man once again in Marxist philosophy. It is assumed here that man can develop a perfect

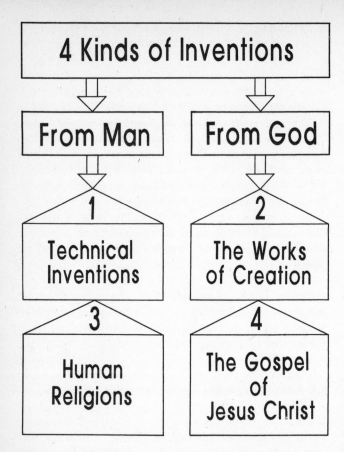

**Figure 12:** *Overview of the Four Types of Inventions and their Source.*

society, under perfect (that is, communist) conditions. We have experienced the dramatic fall of communist ideology in the ex-GDR (German Democratic Republic), since the 9th of November, 1989. *Heimo Schwilk*, commentator for the *Rheinischen Merkur* newspaper, described the events very well in his editorial on the 6th of April, 1990:

"When all possible errors have been committed, we sit abandoned by society', remarked *Bert Brecht* in derision, whose own political errors had to be abandoned. At the end a century in which all sorts of doctrines of salvation and political utopia have been tested, we look back at a confusing storm of ideas. No reasonable ideological life saver appears in sight. After all battles have been fought, reality has triumphed, and a new intellectual humbleness remains. 'If I am supposed to swear by something, I prefer to swear by nothing', expressed *Martin Walser*, sobered, after his dreams of a new national identity burst, due to the profane rush to acquire German marks."

The more easily we recognise that ideologies and philosophies impart a false view of human nature, the harder we look for the true picture of man. Who can we expect to give us an answer, other than the creator who made us. In the area of technology, the builder of a complicated machine is also in the best position to describe its function and nature. The "builder" of man is God. He created a person he could speak with, a being "after our own image" (Gen 1:26). Man was provided with numerous abilities. He was given responsibilities (Gen 1:28), and had a large amount of freedom as God's partner. He had direct fellowship with God and was without blemish and sin.

When we consider ourselves and our fellow man, we must admit honestly: we no longer carry the splendour and glory with which we were bejewelled, we no longer reflect God's characteristics, which man originally had after creation. *Karl Barth* (1886-1968), a Swiss theologian, once described man's being as follows:

"He always comes too early or too late,
he always sleeps, when he should be awake,
he is always aroused, when he should remain calm.
He always remains quiet, when he should speak up,
and always speaks,
when remaining quiet is the only right thing to do.

He always laughs, when he should cry,
and always cries, when he should be able to laugh.
He always wishes to make an exception,
when there are rules to be kept by,
and always subjects himself to a law,
when he could have chosen freedom.
He tinkers around, where only prayer helps,
and always prays, when only action can help.
He always fights, where it is not necessary,
but damaging,
and always speaks of love and peace,
when it is necessary to act aggressively.
He always has the Gospel in his mouth,
when it is more correct
to use a bit of healthy common sense,
and always reasons,
when he should commit himself and others into
God's hands –
there is nothing right about this man,
who the Lord God loves as much as
his only son Jesus Christ,
who He gave to die for us,
so that everything could be made right again."

Something serious and terrible has occurred: man misused the freedom given to him and believed the deceitful offer of Satan that "You will be like God" (Gen 3:5). Man fell in sin and lost fellowship with God as well as his original resemblance to the creator. The current situation of man has been diagnosed by God and described in numerous places in the Bible. Let us understand our defective condition through various passages:

| | |
|---|---|
| Genesis 8:21 | "Never again will I curse the ground because of man, even though every inclination of his heart is evil **from childhood.**" |
| 1 King's 8:46 | "For there **is no-one who does not sin**." |
| Ezra 9:6 | "O my God, I am too ashamed and disgraced |

to lift up my face to you, my God, because our sins are higher than our heads and **our guilt has reached to** the heavens."

| | |
|---|---|
| Ezra 9:15 | "Here we are before you in our guilt, though because of it not one of us can stand in your presence." |
| Job 14:4 | "Who can bring what is pure from the impure? **No-one**!" |
| Job 15:15-16 | "If God places no trust in his holy ones, if even the heavens are **not pure in his eyes**, how much less man, who is vile and corrupt, who drinks up evil like water!" |
| Psalm 14:3 | "All have turned aside, they have together become corrupt; **there is no-one who does good**, not even one." |
| Psalm 38:5 | "My guilt has overwhelmed me like a burden too heavy to bear." |
| Psalm 53:3 | "Everyone has turned away, **they have together become corrupt,**. there is no-one who does good, not even one." |
| Psalm 90:8 | "You have set our iniquities before you, our secret sins in the light of your presence." |
| Psalm 143:2 | "Do not bring your servant into judgment, **for no-one living is righteous before you**." |
| Eccl 7:20 | "There is **not a righteous man on earth** who does what is right and never sins." |
| Isaiah 1:5-6 | "**Your whole head is injured**, your whole heart afflicted. From the sole of your foot to the top of your head there is no soundness." |
| Isaiah 64:6 | "**All** of us have become like one who is unclean, and all our righteous acts are **like filthy rags**." |
| Jeremiah 17:9 | "The heart is deceitful above all things, and beyond cure. Who can understand it?" |
| Jer 30:12-13;17 | "This is what the Lord says: **Your wound is incurable, your injury beyond healing.** There is no-one to plead your cause ... but I will restore you to health and heal your wounds." |

| Nahum 1:3 | "Before the Lord is **no man unguilty**." |
| Matthew 15:19 | "For out of the heart come evil thoughts, murder, adultery, sexual immorality, theft, false testimony, slander." |
| Romans 3:23 | "For **all have sinned**, and fall short of the glory of God." |
| 1 John 1:8 | "If we claim to be without sin, we deceive ourselves and the truth is not in us." |

God's **view of man, presented in the Bible**, rejects all humanistic, marxistic and other ideological claims as false and shows us man as a being created in God's image, with great dignity, with a free will, and with great responsibility. Since the fall of man in Eden, man finds himself in a fallen state towards God and, from his basic nature, tends to do wrong towards man and God.


## 5.2  The Results of Sin: The Three-Fold Death

God is holy. He is absolutely pure. He is light, and therefore God's general judgment on sinful man is: DEATH. God said to the first human beings: "For when you eat of it you will surely die" (Gen 2:17). Man was disobedient and fell under death's judgment: "The wages of sin is death" (Rom 6:23). This line of death is illustrated in the lower part of *Figure 13* and represents a *three-fold death* which affects all of humanity.

**1. The spiritual death**: As an immediate consequence of sinning, man suffers *spiritual death*. This means the separation of fellowship from God, due to *the sin of one man*, and this still affects us: "Therefore, just as sin entered the world through one man, and death through sin, and i this way death came to all men, because all sinned" (Rom 5:12). The Lord Jesus speaks of this death in Matthew 8:22: "Let the (spiritually) dead bury their (physically) own dead!" *Paul* wrote, "You were dead in your transgressions and sins" (Eph 2:1) and meant the spiritual death, which is found in *everyone* by nature.

**2. The physical death**: Another effect of the fall of man was physical death: "... until you return to the ground, since from it you were taken" (Gen 3:19). The above words from Romans 5:12 also characterise physical death as a consequence of spiritual death. The latter occurs with the termination of the biological functions of the body. However, existence does not terminate at that point (Luke 16:19-31). One is merely separated from all that is earthly, since the dead have "Never again will they have a part in anything that happens under the sun." (Eccl 9:6). According to the theory of evolution, death is a necessary prerequisite for higher development. In this sense, *W. Tanner* [T1] expressed the following: "The existence of death has significantly accelerated the process of evolution. It may be of some comfort that without death we humans would probably not yet be in existence." The basis for such a statement was expressed by the microbiologist *R. W. Kaplan* [K1, 236]: "Programmed death in organisms with sexual processes has still another function: the limited duration of life, and, therefore, also limited sexual activity, restricts the exchange of genes between generations, that is, between 'old-fashioned' ancestors and 'progressive' off-spring. Aging and death hinder back-crossing and support evolutionary progress. The built-in aging process and death are indeed painful for the individual, especially humans, but it is the price to be paid so that evolution could produce our species at all." What a terrible error this view of death is, in view of the Biblical testimony.

**3. Eternal death**: The materialistic opinion, that after physical death everything is over, is unmasked as a lie in light of Biblical statements. The Marxist *August Bebel* (1840-1913) was not so sure of himself: "If there is actually a God indeed, we have been real idiots. "The third member of the death chain is *eternal death*. The book of Hebrews describes the passing from physical death to judgment (9:27): "Just as man is destined to die once, and after that to face judgment." When the unredeemed man experiences judgment, he will learn that "It is a dreadful thing to fall into the hands of the living God" (Hebr 10:31). The wrath of God falls on him, since "through the

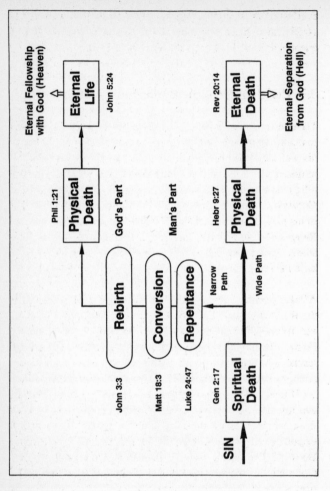

**Figure 13**. *Three-fold death (wide path) and the way of life (narrow path).*

offense of one judgment came upon all men to condemnation" (Rom 5:18). The Bible describes this lost state in many ways: second death, lake of fire (Rev 20:14), eternal fire (Matt 25:41), everlasting destruction (2 Thess 1:9), a place of torment (Luke 16:28); and a place where the worm does not die nor is the fire quenched (Mark 9:44); it is the place of hell (Matt 11:23).

## 5.3  Religions from the Biblical Perspective

The question arises whether there is a way to get off of this path to death. Man has thought a great deal about this and, through his well-described inventive gifts, has thought up thousands of religious ideas. There is a common but incorrect view that all religions actually lead to the same goal. The German poet *Gotthold Ephraim Lessing* (1729-1781) had developed this idea in his play "Nathan the Wise" (Nathan der Weise). The famous *Ringparabel,* in which a Christian, a Jew, and a Muslim appear as discussion partners, would let us believe that all religions have the same saving power.

**A false parable**: The equality of all religions is expressed in the following story: God lives on the top of a high mountain, and the people find themselves at the foot of the mountain. From different sides, people attempt to scale the mountain, to reach God. Many ways are attempted. On one side someone attempts the way of Buddhism, at another place, Islam, others try Hinduism. Many possibilities are attempted. Well-meaning and tolerant, an observer finally said: It really doesn't matter from which side of the mountain the climb is attempted; eventually they will all meet at the top. Is this view correct? Does it deliver a true picture? Remaining within this imagery, God said: this mountain is not scalable by any man through his own strength, no matter how he attempts it. "God lives in unapproachable light, whom noone has seen or can see" (1 Tim 6:16). God has, through Himself, made the way, and he has, through Jesus, climbed down to us at the foot of the mountain. It is stated about him in Luke 1:78-79: "Because of the tender mercy of our God, by which the rising sun will come to us from heaven to shine on those living in darkness and in the shadow of death, to guide our feet into the path of peace."

If some religion could save us, God would have mentioned it. This has not been reported anywhere in the Bible. The Bible describes religious ceremonies and worship of objects in all religions as *idol worship*, *idolatry*, and *sorcery*. Through idol worship, the invisible, living God is replaced by visible representations of human or animal forms, or stars (Deut 4:16-19). God does not wish to give glory to any idols (Isaiah 42:8), and thus all forms of idol worship are condemned:

> "Ye shall have no idols nor carved image, neither rear you up a standing image, neither shall ye set up any image of stone in your land, to bow down unto it; for I am the Lord your God" (Lev 26:1).

In Isaiah 41:29, all religious efforts are said to be in vain:

> "Behold, they are all vanity; their works are nothing; their melted and cast images are wind and confusion."

*Thomas Schirrmacher* summarised the Biblical view of religions with the following relevant statement [S2, 28]: "All religions are, according to the Bible, atheistical, since their gods are only inventions and in reality do not exist."

In the New Testament, marriage is used as an analogue to the intimacy between the Lord Jesus Christ and the Church (Eph 5:23-25). Adultery, harlotry and prostitution are perversion and distortion of marriage. In the same manner, idolatry is described as a perversion of the relationship with the Lord and is described as adultery, harlotry (Ezek 23:27), and prostitution (Hosea 5:4; Rev 17:5). Do the many religious ways with their idolatry lead to heaven? In the New Testament the sin of idolatry is mentioned among those sins which exclude one from the kingdom of God:

> "Know ye not that the unrighteous shall **not** inherit the kingdom of God? Be not deceived: neither fornicators, nor **idolaters**, nor adulterers, nor effeminate, nor abusers of themselves with mankind, nor thieves, nor coveters, nor

drunkards, nor revilers, nor extortioners, shall inherit the kingdom of God." (1 Cor 6:9-10).

"Now the works of the flesh are manifest, which are these: adultery, fornication, uncleanness, lasciviousness, **idolatry**, **sorcery**, hatred, strife, jealousy, wrath, factions, seditions, heresies, envyings, murders, drunkenness, revelings, and the like ... they shall not inherit the kingdom of God." (Gal 5:19-21).

"For *outside* are ... the sorcerers ... and the idolaters." (Rev 22:15).

"But the cowardly, the unbelieving, the vile, the murderers, the sexually immoral, those who practise magic arts, the idolaters and all liars – their place will be in the fiery lake of burning sulphur. This is the second death" (Rev 21:8).

"Nothing impure will ever enter it, nor will anyone who does what is shameful or deceitful, but only those whose names are written in the Lamb's book of life" (Rev 21:27).

All religions are merely glimmering mirages in the desert of lost mankind. To someone dying of thirst, a delusion of water does not help at all. In the same manner, all tolerance towards the human religious fantasies leads to perdition: "There is a way that seems right to a man, but in the end it leads to death" (Prov 14:12). Why does man so often prefer false ways? The German doctor and author *Peter Bamm* (1897-1975) answered in this manner [B1]: "Man loves to worship that which will ruin him."

With respect to religions, *Lutz v. Padberg* made the following summary [P2, 44]:

"From Biblical findings, it is false doctrine to believe that other religions offer an 'alternate way of salvation', since they are conceived and developed as anti-Christ ... Man's revolt against the status assigned to him, that of being

57

human and not God-like superhumans (See Genesis 3:22), leads him to pervert the Biblical representation of God and man. Man does not want to recognise the truth of the creator and tries to reverse the course of events of creation, literally perverting it: He no longer wishes to remain in God's image, but makes God in his human image. That is the origin of religions, which, therefore, include many Christian components, since their foundation is based on what Paul mentioned as 'what may be known of God' (Rom 1:19)."

**Something to keep in mind:** In light of the Bible and in view of salvation from eternal death, religions of all sorts (see Definition **D1**, Chap 4.2) are proven to be perpetual motion machines. Man seeks through perpetual motion machines to overcome the *Law of Conservation of Energy* [1], but that is never possible. Some men make attempts – intentionally or mistakenly – to use religions to overcome the Gospel with the same amount of effort and time others have invested in creating a perpetual motion machine. But it is simply impossible, since Jesus stated, "No one comes to the father but by me" (John 14:6).

## 5.4 The Declaration of God's Will: The Offer of Love

By viewing the *universe,* we can determine *that there is a God.* Upon closer inspection, after recognising the effectiveness

---

[1] *Law of Conservation of Energy*: This important law of nature, which is also known as the First Law of Thermodynamics, was formulated in 1842 by the German medical doctor *Robert Meyer* (1814-1879) and states that in the observable world, energy cannot be created nor destroyed. This law is not an axiom, but a law based on experience, as all laws of nature. The total energy of a system and its environment remains constant in every chemical and physical process, and thus the total energy of the universe remains constant. Energy can neither be created nor destroyed, but only converted into other forms. The Law of Conservation of Energy can also be formulated as the impossibility of creating a perpetual motion machine: It is impossible to build a machine which can operate forever once set in motion, without having to pump more energy into it.

which has been achieved and the ingenuity which was applied during creation, we can conclude that God has great wisdom and power. We cannot extract other characteristics of God from nature. We must now determine whether God has provided us in some way with any other kind of information. Indeed, additional information does come from God: it is the Word of God revealed to us in the form of the Bible. It is the **only** written information God has given us, and the only information authorised by him (2 Peter 1:20-21; 2 Tim 3:16). *Figure 14* illustrates the large gap between the holy God and sinful man, which God Himself has bridged. The information from God answers all important questions about God and ourselves. Here, and only here, do we learn the truth about **where we came from**, **why** we live, and **where we are going**. This information from God peaks in the Gospel of Jesus Christ. In contrast, human information exists in the form of religions. All the religions together do not have the ability to bridge the gap between man and the holy God. The difference between religion and the Gospel is also expressed in *Figure 14* by the different directions of the information arrows. God has informed us that He is a God of righteousness, who hates sin and has established the unavoidable judgment and punishment for sin as eternal death. He is also, however, a God of *love* (1 John 4:16), *goodness* (Lam 3:22) and *mercy* (Eph 2:4), and does not wish that man be lost forever. God shares his intentions with us in several places:

"I will ransom them from the power of sheol; I will redeem them from death. O death, I will be thy plagues; O sheol, I will be thy destruction" (Hosea 13:14).

"Do I take any pleasure in the death of the wicked? declares the Sovereign LORD. Rather, am I not pleased when they turn from their ways and live?" (Ezek 18:23).

"Who will have all men to be saved, and to come unto the knowledge of the truth" (1 Tim 2:4).

"For the Son of man is come to seek and to save that which was lost" (Luke 19:10).

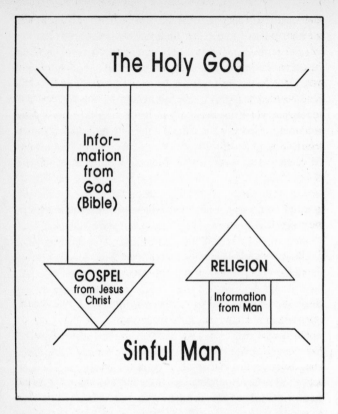

**Figure 14:** *The great difference between religion and the Gospel: the source of information from the Gospel and religion as well as their effectiveness.*

These are clear and unambiguous declarations of God's intentions. Since hell, death, and the Devil cannot be conquered through any human means, God did this Himself through His indescribable and sacrificial love: The fine for our sins was paid on the cross of Golgotha. Jesus Christ Himself, the son of God, stepped into the gap between God and man. No one else could do so, since only He was sinless, and only this sacrifice satisfied God's righteousness. The price for sin could not be paid for through bars of gold, treasures of silver and diamonds, nor human deeds, but rather the price was immeasurable: *the blood of Jesus Christ*! Had it been possible to rescue us without the events at Golgotha, God would have certainly done so. He would not have sacrificed his beloved Son (Matt 3:17), had there been a cheaper way. We can recognise now that there is no religion which can match what God has done. God has done everything necessary for our salvation through the death and resurrection of Jesus. The victory is **achieved** through Jesus: "O death, where is thy sting? O grave, where is thy victory?" (1 Cor 15:55).

In which case would we assess God's love as greater, if through the giving of his son:

- all men would be able to be saved, or if
- only a single person would be able to accept salvation?

Unquestionably, the love must be much greater in the second case, and God knew, of course, in advance how many people would decide (Eph 1:4). We agree with the Bavarian bishop *Hermann Bezzel*, who once said, that God's love is so immeasurable, that He would have sacrificed His only Son, if, according to God's foreknowledge, only a *single person* would be converted. The Bible indicates that the number of redeemed is very large (Rev 7:9), however, it is only a small part of the human race (Matt 7:13). We cannot conclude anything else from the witness of the Scriptures. The Bible states that unequivocally. Many preachers deal with this question with cloudy statements, so as not to restrict at all "God's love". We find God's love to be greatest, if God carried out the rescue operation, even though He knew that only a small percentage would accept the Gospel. We cannot agree with the logic of the "all-will-eventually-be-saved" doctrine, which means that the cost of the crucifixion was not worthwhile.

God's intentions, His action and the coupling of our eternal abode with a personal decision with respect to Jesus Christ, are summarised in John 3:16. Therefore, *C. H. Spurgeon* called this verse the polar star of the Bible: "*For God so loved the world, that He gave His only begotten Son, that whosoever believeth on Him, should not perish but have everlasting life.*" Therefore, in addition to the death line in *Figure 13,* there is also a line of life, which God Himself has made. The question is raised, whether there are many lines of life, which somehow all flow to God, or whether there is only a single way. To avoid answering this question using our own human speculation and wishful thinking, we must pay attention to the information God has given us.

## 5.5  The Way of Salvation to Life: A Way Without Alternatives

The Bible testifies that the path of salvation through Jesus Christ is a unique one, which demands faith, and it reveals all human concepts of salvation as false paths leading to perdition. The exclusiveness of salvation through Christ has always disturbed people, leading occasionally to objections such as the following:

- The people with other religions are also sincere. In sincerity they perform their prayers and offerings and trust fully in their religion. Surely, God also sees it that way. If God is a God of love, he would recognise the sincerity too.

- We try to get along with different religions and agree with the words of the Prussian king *Frederick the Great* (1712-1786): "Each should be blessed after his own manner" . The Gospel, on the other hand, is highly intolerant and demands exclusiveness, when it speak of the path to salvation.

These and similar thoughts are human views, based undoubtedly on good will. The issue here, however, is not *good-will* but *knowledge of the subject matter*. We would like to make the situation clearer through the example of a patient who goes to the doctor because of stomach pains. The doctor diagnoses an inflamed appendix and orders an operation as the only cure possible. What would we say about the patient's suggestions that the doctor should consider other means, such as chamomile tea, fizz tablets, three days vacation or a thorough stomach massage? Is it close-minded to ignore the suggestions of the patient? Without the operation, the patient will die, even if he drinks chamomile tea in total sincerity. Only the expert, the doctor, knows which is correct to save lives.

It is also that way with God. He is the only expert in the matter of sin. As Lord, and doctor, he communicates to us that there is only a single means of salvation, namely, the Gospel of Jesus Christ. The uniqueness and exclusiveness can be found in numerous places:

"I am the Lord, and besides me there is no saviour" (Isaiah 43:11).

"He that believeth and is baptised shall be saved; but he that believeth not shall be damned" (Mark 16:16).

"Whoever believes in the Son has eternal life, but whoever rejects the Son will not see life, for God's wrath remains on him" (John 3:36).

"Salvation is found in no-one else, for there is **no other name** under heaven given to men by which we must be saved" (Acts 4:12).

"He who has the Son has life; he who does not have the Son of God does not have life" (1 John 5:12).

"I am the way and the truth and the life. **No-one** comes to the Father except through me" (John 14:6).

"For no-one can lay any foundation other than the one already laid, which is Jesus Christ" (1 Cor 3:11).

In view of these precise and unambiguous statements, we are sinning, if we teach any other way to salvation. This exclusive claim on the part of Jesus Christ is the natural continuation of the first Commandment in the Old Testament (Exodus 20:2-3). God told us clearly in His Word, that there is **only one way** to life. Since eternal life is at stake, it would be criminally foolish to follow the broad path. We should be grateful for the generous offer of a chance to be saved and follow this way in obedience and belief.

## 5.6 The Way to Life: A Command from God

It is God's explicit will to help us gain eternal life. Whether we choose eternal life or eternal death, is our decision, but God wishes that we simply accept eternal life: "I have set before you life and death, blessing and cursing; therefore, choose life, that both thou and thy seed may live" (Deut 30:19). In short: it is a matter of heaven or hell. The call for eternal life is a "holy call" (2 Tim 1:9) and is a direct command: "Lay hold on eternal life, unto which thou art also called" (1 Tim 6:12). God sent His son to the world with this command: "The Father, who sent me, he gave me a commandment, what I should say, and what I should speak ... *his commandment* is *life everlasting*" (John 12:49-50). *Heinrich Kemner* [K3, 11] wrote about this offer: "When God calls, it is not the membrane of our understanding which is moved, but that of our heart." God's call should be taken as a command which is unavoidable, since our eternity is at stake. Those who make the wrong decision and do not take the proper action here, will have no opportunity to make corrections on the other side. Eternity can not bring back what one turned down in a second. Do all men obey God's loving command? A sad description of the decision made by most people is given to us in John 3:19: "They loved darkness more than the light." This makes God's call even more urgent: "Strive to enter in at the narrow gate!" (Luke 13:24). Most people, however, follow the line of death (*Figure 13*, lower), which leads to damnation, but the Lord calls with an urgent warning: "Enter through the narrow gate. For wide is the gate and broad is the road that leads to destruction, and many enter through it. But small is the gate and narrow the road that leads to life, and only a few find it" (Matt 7:13-14). We will deal in Chapter 6 with the important question, how one enters through the narrow gate.

## 5.7  The Way to Life: Paid for at Golgotha

God humbled Himself to the lowest level at the cross of Jesus Christ. God judged sin there. The greatest rescue mission in the world's history took place there. The son of God left heaven and took on the form of a servant: "He humbled himself and became obedient unto death, even the death of the cross" (Phil 2:8). *H. W. Beck* describes the situation well [B2, 61]: "At the cross there was no actor who skillfully played the role of a doomed man – it was not some example for the many martyrs of various ideologies and utopias! No: the man at the cross was uninterchangeably God." Seven hundred years before the historical facts, God reported it all through the prophet Isaiah:

"He was despised and rejected by men, a man of sorrows, and familiar with suffering. Like one from whom men hide their faces he was despised, and we esteemed him not. Surely took up our infirmities and carried our sorrows, yet we considered him stricken by God, smitten by him, and afflicted. But he was pierced *for our transgressions*, he was crushed for our iniquities; the punishment that brought us peace was upon him, and *by his wounds we are healed*. We all, like sheep, have gone astray, each of us has turned to his own way; and the LORD has laid on him *the iniquity of us all*!" (Isaiah 53:3-6).

It is made clear here that the gap between God and man, caused by sin is very deep. Only one person was in a position to step into this gap and fill it, and – God be praised – he did so out of love towards us. At the cross, Jesus identified Himself with the sin of the world, allowing himself to be punished for the sin.

Here we see that there is no cheaper way to get rid of sin. It will not be possible to find a cure for sin, such as those against hair loss or headaches. For our sin, there is only **one** solution: God heaped all sin on Jesus and thus provided us with the possibility to be freed of sin: "God made him who had no sin to be sin for us, so that in him we might become the righteousness of God" (2 Cor 5:21). Unlike the Son of God, we not only know sin, but we also do it. But Jesus *was made sin* at the cross, that is, our sins were laid on Him, and He was punished on our behalf. Since the only payment for sin was made there, only the righteousness provided through Jesus' cross counts. Therefore the cross of Golgotha is God's one and only offer to all mankind. God's price for us was immeasurably high, He gave His most valuable possession: his son Jesus Christ. The price here had nothing to do with gold or silver, but the redemption was carried out "with the precious blood of Christ, as of a lamb without blemish and without spot" (1 Peter 1:19). The single-ness and uniqueness of the work of redemption is found in the person of Jesus. This can be expressed in a concise formula: "Saying YES to Jesus, we attain eternity. Saying NO, we lose it. Two words determine our eternal fate! There is **only a single place** in this world where God's judgment doesn't apply, and that is under the cross:

- Nowhere else is there grace!
- Nowhere else is there salvation!
- Nowhere else can we obtain such blessings!

Only if we are aware of our sins, can we clearly understand the full consequences of the cross. The Holy Spirit convicts us of being sinners (John 16;8-9).

An illustration may help clarify the salvation provided through Golgotha: During the dry season in the savannah of Africa and on the prairies of North America, devastating fires often break out. The fires advance with great speed and destroys all animals and people in their path. What should be done when one sees the roaring fire approaching? One quickly lights a fire to create a fire break, a burned-out surface. When the blazing avalanche rolls in, one is in a secure place, since there is no more fuel for the fire there. The sparks fall harmlessly in this area. This burned-out surface is an analogy of the cross. God has judged sin here. Here the righteous one has suffered once and for all for the unrighteous. Golgotha is the city of refuge. Those that flee to it no longer fall under the judgment of God.

At the cross:
- Jesus was made poor, so that we could be made rich;
- Jesus was made homeless and gave us a home;
- Jesus carried our suffering, so that we could be made free;
- Jesus suffered thirst, so that we would never again be thirsty;
- Jesus carried our disgrace, so that He could be our righteousness.

With the message of the cross, God satisfied neither our need to understand nor our wish for visible signs, but here God offered his rescuing power: "For the preaching of the cross is to them that perish foolishness; but unto us who are saved it is the power of God" (1 Cor 1:18). At the cross, all our wisdom melts away; here all human attempts at salvation through religion and philosophies are destroyed. *Heinrich Kemner* formulated it well: "When one honestly and sincerely comes to the cross of Jesus Christ, one can learn and experience more about God in a single minute than all the science of this world can ever prove. The knowledge of God is not lacking reason, but is rather above reason." Through the cross, God has provided the only possibility for salvation forever. Even when it seems to someone that God's way is foolishness, it doesn't change the saving power for those who accept it. Two Old Testament events should help make clear how God provided only a **single way** for salvation and also show that it is not a matter of human understanding.

**1. The Ark:** During the Flood, God offered only a *single possibility* for salvation from the approaching judgment upon the unbelievers: *Noah's Ark.* Let us view the situation at that time. People could only grin condescendingly, when *Noah* said he was taking precautions to save himself from God's judgment. He did not build his huge ship near a harbour, but rather near the forest. He made no provisions for a rudder nor sail for his extraordinary construction. People found the motive for building this ship, as well as the location and form, utter nonsense. Then came the Flood. The critics began then to try to save themselves. They climbed into their boats, climbed up trees and onto houses, and fled to the mountains, but there was no place they could be saved: "All flesh died" (Gen 7:21). Salvation was only possible through the means devised by God. It is also that way with the Cross. Salvation is possible only in this way. Through all other means one is lost. The issue here is not what most people hold to be true. Many people would have had room in the ark, however, only very few, namely, eight people, were saved. The power of the cross is so great, that all people **could** be saved through it. However, **only those** who have actually "climbed" into this New Testament ark will be rescued.

**2. The raised serpent** (Num 21): During the wanderings in the desert after leaving Egypt, the people of Israel grumbled about God. Then God sent *fiery serpents* into the camp. This was a horrible event, and many died, since the serpent's poison was deadly. The message of salvation from God was very simple: "Make a snake and put it up on a pole; anyone who is bitten can look at it and live" (Num 21:8). In other words: don't look at the wounds nor at the danger, but look only at God's sign. In this sign there was salvation and help, since God had committed himself with his word. Many probably mocked and considered such measures against reason. They probably had their own counter-measures: cold packs, burning the wounds, sucking out the poisoned blood, but all their own "reasonable" ways did not help: they died! Others obeyed God, looked at the given sign, and remained alive.

A good 1000 years later, Jesus' discussion with *Nicodemus* occurred. Jesus explained to him that the iron serpent was a foreshadow of his cross: "Just as Moses lifted up the snake in the desert, so the Son of Man must be lifted up, that everyone who believes may have eternal life in him" (John 3:14-15).

**What we should keep in mind:** We should look on Jesus' cross. Only there can one obtain eternal life. There the required price was paid. Only this currency was acceptable to God. It is God's sign of salvation. *Heinrich Kemner* emphasised (periodical "Erweckliche Stimme", 8/1979): "God's hands on the cross invite us all. But one only receives the wedding invitation, when one has the honesty to accept the judgment of God placed on his son at the cross."

# 6 The Path to Life: How to Find It and Stay on It

God has provided a path to salvation, and has described exactly how we can find this path. Still man could not suppress his nature and has been active in thinking up alternative ways to salvation:

- Some claim there is a single church able to sanctify; only those who belong to it and follow its rites can go to heaven. According to the statements of the New Testament (NT), the true church, the body of Christ, consists of *all* born-again Christians. This has nothing to do with nominal membership in a church. Of course, every believer will endeavour to gather with other Christians in his area, who also try to apply the NT principles of fellowship. That requires, of course, an interest in the Bible!

- Sects claim, among other things, that only their church can save. Many a seeker is thus deceived and believes to have attained admittance to heaven by joining a church and performing certain deeds.

- Others believe that actions such as baptism, the Lord's Supper, confirmation or communion are entrance tickets to heaven. That is a serious error. We don't deny that baptism and the Lord's Supper are good, since baptism was instituted by Jesus himself as a step of obedience for the believers and the Supper is a central activity in the fellowship among Christians. But baptism and the Lord's Supper are in no way effective to save.

- Good works are pleasing to God (2 Tim 3:17; James 2:17), but they too lack the power to save (2 Tim 1:9). As someone lay dying, he asked the pastor to come to him, to take the Lord's Supper. Afterwards he donated a large sum of money for missionary work and then thought nothing could happen to him with respect to his eternal destination. It is widely believed that the Lord's Supper and good works have saving power.

We must classify the examples mentioned above as religious acts, even though they have a Christian appearance. The ways of religion do not have saving power, only the Gospel does. Therefore, we wish to look at the Biblical message carefully which describes what the way God prescribed for salvation. The way to eternal life for everyone who listens to the Gospel is marked by three milestones or stations (*Figure 13*), which cannot be substituted or avoided by detouring: They are described by the key words *repentance*, *conversion* and *rebirth*. Man must recognise his lost state, repent and become converted, then God will respond by giving man the gift of rebirth. There are numerous church members, who consider themselves Christians, but have never experienced repentance and rebirth. According to the Biblical witness they are not saved. What a huge disappointment there will be, when on the Day of Judgment the Lord says to them: "I never knew you" (Matt 7:23). Therefore, we want to consider carefully the way of salvation prescribed by the Lord.

## 6.1 Repentance: A Thorough Change in Thinking

The New Testament concept of repentance (Greek *metanoia*) means a thorough change of mind, a fundamental rethinking, a clearing out of old views, opinions and ideas. This inner process of rethinking is clarified through the example of the Prodigal Son: "I will set out and go back to my father and say to him, Father, I have sinned against heaven, and against you" (Luke 15:18). To understand the characteristics, effects, and necessity of repentance, we will let several portions of Scripture speak for themselves:

Out of kindness to us, God provided the possibility to repent: "God's kindness leads you towards repentance" (Rom 2:4). God wishes to rescue us from eternal perdition (2 Peter 3:9;

Matt 3:2). Only those who repent can enter God's kingdom. Therefore, repentance is a command ordered by God (Matt 3:2; Acts 17:30). God sent his Son to this world to call sinners to repentance (Luke 5:32). Therefore, Jesus began his first sermon with the words: "Repent and believe the Gospel" (Mark 1:15).

Repentance is for man a personal, free decision (Luke 15:18). Repentance is a *necessary step* to escape eternal perdition: "But unless you repent, you too will all perish" (Luke 13;3). God wants us to be saved: "The Lord ... is not wanting anyone to perish, but everyone to come to repentance" (2 Peter 3:9). Whoever refuses to repent, will experience what was expressed by *Ludwig Thimme*: "Without repentance and conversion there is no escape from hell."

The Irish poet, *C. S. Lewis* (1898-1963), described the necessity of repentance as follows [L3, 18]: "The one who turns back first is further ahead. The sooner I begin to replan a task falsely begun, the sooner I arrive at my goal ... A glance at the present situation of the world shows us quite clearly, that humanity must have made some great error. We are on the wrong path and must turn back. In this case too, such a turn would be the fastest way to make progress."

Repentance is the prerequisite to conversion; it is the turning point where one can turn away from the wide path of damnation and, at the same time, the entrance gate for the narrow path to life. Through repentance, we recognise that we are lost before God, admit our sins to the Lord Jesus Christ (1 John 1:8-9), and receive forgiveness for **all** our sins. Repentance is the conscious turning away from our own will and toward the will of God. If the repentance is real, it leads to conversion: "Repent, then, and turn to God" (Acts 3:19).

## 6.2 Conversion: The Conscious Turn to God

Repentance and conversion are closely coupled with one another. Both belong together, since conversion is the conscious first move toward God. The parable of the Prodigal Son (Luke 15:20) describes the following event: "So he got up and went to his father. But while he was still a long way off, his father saw him and was filled with compassion for him; he ran to his son, threw his arms around him and kissed him". If one takes a step towards the Lord, the Lord will come a thousand steps towards him. A turn towards God is always met with acceptance from God. Everyone is invited. Since there is no exception, *Heinrich Kemner* said [K2, 11]: "You can come, as you are: with poisoned imaginations, with sinful life, with ... You can come from the enemy of your soul, from the husks of the Prodigal Son!"

Since there is often misunderstanding with respect to conversion, we want to discuss this second step to eternal life using common questions:

### 6.2.1  Is Conversion Necessary to Attain Eternal Life?

According to the witness of the Scriptures, conversion is an essential step to escape from death. In the Old Testament, we have already read:

> "But if a wicked man turns away from all the sins ... he will surely *live*; he will *not die*" (Ezek 18:21).

> "Do I take any pleasure in the death of the wicked (eternally!) ? declares the Sovereign Lord. Rather, am I not pleased when they *turn* from their ways and *live*?" (Ezek 18:23)

> "*Repent* and live!" (Ezek 18:32).

The Lord Jesus also teaches that without conversion **no one** will see the kingdom of God: "I tell you the truth, unless you change and become like little children, you will never enter the kingdom of heaven" (Matt 18:3). Conversion is, therefore, an essential step for attaining Life. Whoever neglects it will receive eternal death.

### 6.2.2 How Often Does Conversion Occur?

Many people say one must be converted daily or once a year, or perhaps many times during a lifetime. As we will show, conversion is followed by rebirth. Like physical birth which occurs only once, conversion and rebirth also occur only once in the life of a person. When someone becomes weak in his belief, so that he notices that a correction is necessary, this correction can occur through a "renewal" to the Lord Jesus. This is a repeat of repentance, but not of conversion. The single conversion is generally so decisive an experience that we should be in the position to state (Luke 15:20; 1 Thess 1:9; 1 Peter 2:25; Acts 26:12-18) where and when we consciously took this step. Whoever was raised in a believing family has learned the Biblical doctrine from childhood on and has usually accepted it. They are not spared the step of a **personal** conversion, since God does not have grandchildren, but only children. In such cases, the conversion will not always be an experience with revolutionary consequences, but the affected person can, nevertheless, whole-heartedly pay witness to the fact that he belongs to Jesus.

### 6.2.3 Who Must Be Converted?

This is a key question, since we are personally challenged by it. Commonly one thinks: the godless, the atheists, the nihilists, the communists, the spiritists, the animists, the evolutionists, the adulterers, the Free Masons, the spies, the thieves, the warlocks, and murderers must be converted, but not the church people, the pastors, church leaders, the Evangelists, the Catholics, the Baptists, the God-fearing, etc. According to the Bible, however, **everyone** must converted, that means, the first group mentioned here, as well as the other groups. Even those who believe in God must be converted. Even the demons believe, but they tremble (James 2:19); they have a "certain belief", but, nevertheless, no part of eternal salvation.

A pastor stated before many witnesses that he had a theological education behind him and had already preached several years before a congregation. One day he was reading in the Bible with the purpose of preparing for his sermon. The words gripped him, he kneeled down and entrusted the Lord Jesus with his entire life. That was the hour of his conversion. He claimed, from then on, that as a saved man, he preached in a totally different manner and could provide his congregation with bread instead of stone.

Even those whose prayers have been answered, have not necessarily been converted. The well-known German evangelist *Wilhelm Pahls* described a young man who went to sea. His mother was a believing woman, who told him as he departed: "If you get in danger, then pray!" The young man had already been at high sea for some time when, during some rough weather, he was working on deck and fell from the rocking ship into the foaming sea, without anybody noticing. No one was on deck and could see him. In his trouble, he cried to God and asked for help. Then the unimaginable occurred; the ship turned after some minutes and began looking for him. He was found and saved from sure death. Why was the rescue operation undertaken? The young man discovered, that during the exact second in which he stumbled into the sea, a sailor looked out of a porthole and witnessed the event. He reported it immediately to the captain, and so the search operation began. God heard the prayer of the young man and answered in a wonderful way through the actions of the sailor. He was rescued from drowning, but was he saved for eternity? No! It is known that the young man was converted only later during an evangelisation and thus received eternal salvation. Answers to prayer for unbelievers are a temporary act of mercy by God, a call from God to repentance and conversion. "Do you show not realising that God's kindness leads you towards repentance?" (Rom 2:4). Many soldiers have prayed for protection during the dangers of war. Only a few have been converted. As soon as things went well again with them, they no longer searched for God.

*Peter* had been with Jesus a long time; he experienced the great deeds of God and believed in him, but nevertheless he had not yet been converted. Even Jesus confirmed *Peter's* belief, but his conversion had not yet taken place: "But I have prayed for you, that your faith may not fail. And *when you have turned back*, strengthen your brothers" (Luke 22;32). Faith is a prerequisite for conversion, since one cannot turn to God, if one does not know him at all and have a certain trust in him. In Acts 11:21, we read, "And a great number of people believed and turned to the Lord." Faith and conversion can occur together within a very short time span. We sometimes see this during evangelisations; people hear the Gospel for the first time in its full power, they trust and believe the message, and then come forward to be converted. It is often the case, however, that people are already prepared through reading the Bible and good Christian books, through long contact with practising Christians, through visits to worship services or get-togethers in private homes and are then converted later, when they are ready to give their lives entirely to the Lord. Some have been involved in church work for a long time and believe they are "good Christians", but they were never converted. Whoever remains in such self-delusion is on the track to hell.

**Keep This in Mind:** Everyone who wishes to see God's kingdom must at *sometime* be converted. *Ernst Modersohn* once said, "Even the best upbringing, the most devout disposition does not make a conversion superfluous. Every person must be converted sometime, that is, give his heart and life decisively to the Lord." Only a true conversion can save, it is the necessary step a person must take to attain eternal life. He who neglects it receives eternal death.

### 6.2.4 Why Should One Become Converted?

We have already indicated that a conversion to Jesus Christ is necessary to enter heaven. Anyone who has been converted himself can perform the important service of showing searching people the way to heaven. Jesus not only gave us this "key power", he commissioned us to do this task for him.

**The key to heaven:** The Lord said to *Peter*, "I will give you the keys of the kingdom of heaven" (Matt 16:19). That applies not only to Peter; in fact, all who belong to Jesus can lead other people to the kingdom of heaven. We can show the way to everyone who is searching. We can promise forgiveness to every sinner, "If you forgive anyone his sins, they are forgiven; if you do not forgive them, they are not forgiven" (John 20:23). We have been called upon to open the gate to heaven for others. This key service is not limited to any office. Every disciple of Jesus has this key power. In Revelations 1:18 Jesus spoke of other keys: "I hold the keys of death and Hades." He entrusted no one else with these keys. In this matter, only He had authority. It would not be good, if we had these keys. Otherwise we would bring ourselves and others to hell. Our task is therefore unambiguous: "That one brings the others to heaven", as *Luther* stated.

### 6.2.5 When Should One Become Converted?

Jesus described those who, after hearing about the word, wisely obey it (Matt 7:24). That is especially true about conversion. When the message touches our heart, a decision is demanded: "Today if you hear his voice, do not harden your hearts" (Hebr 4:7). The *eunuch from Ethiopia* came searching in Jerusalem. He bought a roll of scripture, but he did not understand the contents of the message. But when Philip explained the Gospel to him on the basis of the text from Isaiah 53:7-8, he immediately accepted this offer of salvation with his whole heart: he believed in Jesus Christ as the Son of God, he was baptised and went joyously on his way (Acts 8:26-39). We have a good example here: a person heard the message of salvation and accepted it without delay. Another man is reported in Acts who should serve as a counter example. *Festus* also heard about faith in Jesus Christ and other central doctrines of the Bible. His reaction, however, was: "That's enough for now! You may leave. When I find it convenient, I will send for you" (Acts 24:25). We never hear that he called for *Paul* again so that he could be converted. For *Festus* the offered opportunity of grace was probably missed. In our days, also, many people go through missionary tents and other evangelical events without using these opportunities to make a decision.

Many people believe they can be converted shortly before their death. The grace given to the *thief on the cross* who called on the Lord at the last moments of his life should be seen as an exception. We cannot manipulate the time of our conversion as easily as we would perhaps like to. One can only be converted when God calls. *Bezzel* warned [K2, 11] that, "The grace of Jesus is unexhaustable in its forgiving power, but takes place within an unavoidable second." If our end approaches with great weakness, great pain, delirious fever, or suddenly, our chances dwindle to nothing.

The well-known German pastor *Wilhelm Busch* (1897-1966) tells (shortened here) about an experience which causes one to reflect [B5, 25-28]:

I was awaken in the night by a telephone call: A dying man asked for a pastor. I hurried to the hospital. In bed lay a young man. His wife sat distraught next to him. When she saw me, she jumped up: "Pastor, give my husband quickly the Lord's Supper!" Death could be seen in the face of the sick man, who took no notice of me. With my prayers and words of grace, I wished to accompany the man into eternity: "The blood of Jesus Christ cleanse you from all sins ..." He slowly opened his eyes. The wife pressed me once more about the Lord's Supper. I said to her in the corridor: "Do you believe that the outward ceremony can save him from God's judgment? When your husband knows the Lord Jesus Christ as his saviour and believes in him, then he is saved, even if he does not take the Lord's Supper now. And without Jesus the Lord's Supper does not help at all!" She pressed me incessantly; I gave in. After the celebration, the man sank back on the pillows satisfied. I left the room so that the couple could say goodbye. Half an hour later, I entered the room again. An amazing scene: the man sat up in bed and said to us, "I'm over the hill. I'm getting better!" I took the hand of the sick man and said, "Dear man, as you stood at the gates of eternity the Lord Jesus came to you in his mercy. Never leave this saviour!" Then a terrible grin appeared on the face of the man, it was a flicker from hell. Smiling mockingly, he said, "Oh, I no longer need all that. I'm alive again!" I heard this unbelievable statement, horrified. I was speechless. And as I stood there, the patient suddenly grabbed his heart and slowly sank back. He was dead!

A city missionary in Hamburg, Germany, once carried out an unusual survey [L2, 81]. As a pastor in a large hospital, he had written down the names of all those who on their apparent death beds had been converted and then, to everyone's surprise, recovered. He determined that only in rare cases were the conversions real. They were usually only the products of miserable fear. Only "godly sorrow" (2 Cor 7:10) brings true conversion. Sorrow, because one has made God unhappy leads one to turn to him and thus to life. The "sorrow of the world", the unhappiness caused by fear and self-centredness, however, "leads to death." *Paul Le Seur* warned about false orientation [L2, 81]: "Whoever sees death as a magical means to make one holy, without any personal commitment, finds himself in sharp contradiction with the Bible and makes all spiritual welfare, indeed the entire history of salvation, superfluous."

### 6.2.6  In Practical Terms, How Does Conversion Occur?

Upon conversion, we give our entire life over to the Lord Jesus. We allow him to rule our lives. He is the landlord in all the chambers of our being. The Lord pressures no one; he simply stands knocking at the door of our heart (Rev 3:20) and waits, until we invite him in through a very personal prayer, to be lord over our lives. According to John 1:12, this process is followed by becoming a child of God: "Yet to all who received him, to those who believed in his name, he gave the right to become children of God." Perhaps you, the reader, have by now realised that you want to be converted too, but don't know exactly how this occurs. That will be explained next, so that you too can be certain of salvation.

Call on the name of the Lord, that is, pray to Jesus Christ. Maybe you think: What should I say, since I have never spoken to him before. To help, a form-free prayer follows, as an example:

"Dear Jesus Christ, I realise that I am guilty of sin and that I am not worthy to stand before you on judgment day. But you came to the world to save lost sinners like me. You died on the cross; you were punished for my sins, so that I could be cleansed of all sin. I have faith in this. My life is like an open book; you can see my weaknesses, false beliefs, and my past indifference towards you. Please forgive me for my sins, and change the things in me which do not please you. Thank you for doing this now. You are the truth; I know I can rely on you to accept my plea, as you promised in your Word.

Lord, I ask you to fill my life with goodness. Guide me, directly and through your Word, and help me to live my life correctly. Because I know you are the good shepherd, who will protect me, I wish to entrust you with all aspects of my life: my thoughts and actions, my work, my free time, my plans, my friends, my money ... Give me the strength to change my ways of sin. If I fail and accidently sin again, let me recognise my failure and ask for forgiveness. Change my ways to ones which you bless, and improve my attitude towards you and the people I deal with from day to day. Help me to understand your Word in the Bible and to obey you. I want to follow you and have you as **my** Lord. Amen."

If this prayer, or its equivalent, came sincerely out of your heart, then you are now a child of God: "Yet to all who received him (= the Lord Jesus), to those who believed in his name,he gave the right to become the children of God" (John 1:12). The fulfilled life which God promised you has begun. Also, eternal life has been given to you. All of heaven participated in the event of your conversion, since he said in Luke 15:10, "In the same way, I tell you, there is rejoicing in the presence of the angels of God over one sinner who repents (= that is converted)."

Now a few pieces of advise follow, to allow you to get off to a good start as a Christian:

**1. Read the Bible:** Begin to read the Bible every day, to inform yourself about God's will. The Bible is the only book authorised by God. For your new life, reading this book is necessary nourishment. It may be best to begin with one of the Gospels. The Gospel of John is specially appropriate at the beginning.

**2. Pray:** Speak daily to God and to Jesus Christ in prayer. It will give you strength, and it will change you. You can pray about all daily matters: concerns, joys, plans and intentions. Thank the Lord for everything which moves you. By reading the Bible and praying a "spiritual circulation" arises, which is important for a healthy spiritual life.

**3. Seek Fellowship:** Seek and develop contact with other conscientious Christians. When one takes a glowing coal out of a fire, it is extinguished very quickly. Our love for Jesus will grow cool, if not kept burning through fellowship with other believers. Join a Biblically sound congregation and work with it. A good, lively church, where one believes in the whole Bible, is essential for our spiritual life and a healthy growth in faith.

**4. Be Obedient:** While reading the Bible, you will find many helpful directions for all areas of life and your walk with God. Apply what you have learned and you will experience a great blessing. The best way to prove our love for the Lord is through our obedience: "This is love for God: to obey his commands" (1 John 5:3).

**5. Bear Witness:** Tell others what Jesus Christ means to you. Many people have not yet accepted the Gospel. They need our example and witness. Now you can work for God.

Rejoice in the fact that you have consciously accepted to Jesus Christ as saviour and have been accepted by God.

### 6.2.7 What are the Consequence of Conversion?

*Spurgeon* once said, "A true conversion cannot be hidden any more than a light in a dark room." With the conversion goes a change in life, characterised by an abrupt effort to stop sinning. *Paul Humburg* has formulated this change using an analogy with trains: "Before our conversion we sinned right on schedule, but after our conversion, we liken every sin to a train crash." The converted person does not remain sinless, of course, but the significance of sin has been radically changed. The priorities of life change; the kingdom of God now plays the central role. The converted person has a hunger for God's Word, and he seeks fellowship with others who are also converted. He is led by the Holy Spirit (Rom 8:14) and the fruits of the spirit (Gal 5:22) will be made visible for all to see. The conversion is a cut-off point from the old life, and at the same time, the start of a new life. The New Testament explains: "If anyone is in Christ, he is a new creation" (2 Cor 5:17). The conversion has a two-fold effect: our life on earth become more meaningful and, because we become children of God, we also receive the gift of eternal life. *Heinrich Kemner* wrote [K2, 44]: "As you live, you will die. And as you die, you will carry on living. And where you carry on with life is where you will remain." Upon conversion, one is "born again" to become a child of God. This re-birth is discussed in the next chapter.

# 7 Born Again: Birth into the Family of God

The third step in salvation (see *Figure 13*) is being born again. *Schlatter* coined the very relevant phrase: "Conversion is the last act of the old man, rebirth is the first experience of the new man." Rebirth is God's answer to our conversion. In the same way that we could not influence our birth into this world, rebirth is something which happens to us. The process of being born again allows us to avoid being eternally lost. Jesus emphasised: "I tell you the truth, unless a man is born again, he cannot see the kingdom of God" (John 3:3). We can only be saved, if we have been born again.

## 7.1 Characteristics of Being Born Again

- **It is a birth carried out by the spirit of God:** "Flesh gives birth to flesh ... The wind blows wherever it pleases. You hear its sound, but you cannot tell where it comes from or where it is going. So it is with everyone born of the Spirit" (John 3:6,8).

- **It is a birth given by God:** Unlike our natural birth, in being born again no man became a father, but this was effected by God. This aspect is especially clear from John 1:13: "Who were born, not of blood, nor of the will of the flesh, nor of the will of man, but of God."

- **It is a birth which occurs through God's word:** "For you have been born again, not of perishable seed, but of imperishable, through the living and enduring word of God" (1 Peter 1:23).

- **It is a birth into the family of God:** Through our natural birth, we become a child of our *earthly* father; by being born again, we become a child of the *heavenly* father.

## 7.2 False Views of Being Born Again

**1. Being born again should not be confused with baptism:**
If child baptism were the same as being born again, then 95%
of the population of the Western part of Germany would be
children of God. *Hitler*, *Stalin* and *Mussolini* would also be
saved. The well-known evangelical pastor *Wilhelm Busch*
warned us about this erroneous thinking [B4, 141]: "... this is
due to the misleading teaching about baptism. Should a
conscience ever be troubled, should a person ever come to the
conclusion that he, like the prodigal son, must change, should
the spirit of God ever awaken a heart, then it will be immediately numbed by the message: you have already been baptised.
Everything is okay. Then the awakened conscience relaxes
again." This widely-spread teaching of *"baptism rebirth"*
belongs to the false doctrines of our times with the most serious
consequences.

**2. Being born again is not reincarnation:** At first *Nicodemus*
thought the words of Jesus, "Unless a man is born again" (John
3:3) referred to a physical rebirth: "How can a man be born
when he is old? Surely he cannot enter a second time into his
mother's womb to be born!" (John 3:4). Today many people,
influenced by esoteric teachings and far-eastern religions believe in a physical reincarnation. No place in the Bible speaks
about such an event. It teaches rather: "Just as man is destined *to
die once*, and after that to face judgment" (Hebr 9:27).

**3. Being born again is not a matter of Christian upbring-
ing:** It is a great blessing when our children are raised in Christian families, hearing God's Word at an early age and learning
how the Bible tells us to behave. However, such children are
not necessarily born again. God does not have grandchildren,
only children, who become so by being born again. The world-
famous evangelist *Billy Graham* expressed this thought well:
"If you are born in a garage, you are by no means a car. If
your are born in a Christian family, you are by no means a
Christian."

**4. One is not born again through church membership:** If we belong to Christ, according to the Bible, it is assumed that we will join a church fellowship which is true to the Bible. When a new believer asked the evangelist whether he could be a Christian all by himself, he was given an appropriate answer: "You can try to row across the Atlantic in a rubber dingy but the probability is very great that you will be caught by the waves in a storm and not reach the other shore. Likewise, without a lively fellowship you won't reach your goal."

## 7.3 The Results of Being Born Again

We have discussed the three decisive and necessary steps to man's salvation. Whoever has consciously made a personal decision for Jesus Christ to follow this path has become a rich man indeed. The greatest inheritance a man can receive awaits him. He will spend eternity in the company of God. Heaven is his imperishable inheritance. In contrast to the path of death in the lower part of *Figure 13*, physical death now leads to life. The reality of Philippians 1:21 now applies to this path of life: "For to me to live is Christ, and to die is gain."

The Gospel is the best news ever proclaimed. It is the message of God's love towards us, the message of joy and salvation. It is the message which brings us to heaven. Whoever comes personally to Jesus, our Lord, in repentance and conversion, is saved. But the message also has another effect. One can hear God's call and ignore it. Whoever has heard God's call and not accepted it, has judged himself. That person remains in his own guilt and cannot escape judgment (Hebr 9:27; John 3:36b). The damning judgment of sin remains upon the unsaved man. If we don't turn to Jesus, we will be eternally lost, even with a Christian tradition. Religion has only an anaesthetic effect, but no saving power. Viewing religion in this way, *Karl Marx* was right in saying that, "Religion is the opiate of the masses." If we accept God's call and convert to Jesus Christ, then we have been healed, the sun of eternity has arisen, we have been led from death to life (John 5:24). Jesus is the end of all religion! We must decide between religion and the Gospel.

An analogy: During May 1990, as we were driving to an evangelisation lecture in Hungary, we needed to go through the Plabutsch tunnel in Austria. Since this tunnel is 9919 metres long, it is among the longest in the world (the very longest: St. Gotthard/Alps, 16.32 km long) and driving through it seemed endless. At the end, there were two exits. One went in the direction of South Graz and the other towards Vienna-Klagenfurt. This trip through the tunnel provided me with an analogy:

Many of us consider our death as a kind of dark tunnel, and many ask themselves whether the tunnel has an exit. Yes, at the end of the long tunnel there is an exit into another "world". We come out either on the street of eternal life or on the path of eternal death. We must all go through this "tunnel of death", but the decision as to where we will exit is made before entering the tunnel.

# 8 Belief from the Heart: The Saving Rope

In the preceding chapters we discussed the steps necessary for salvation, which are repentance, conversion and being born again. Little was mentioned about faith, although this is also of fundamental importance for salvation. Conversion and being born again are occurrences, which usually links them to a specific time and place; faith, however, is a state of being of the saved person. Salvation comes through it. This process was explained picturesquely by *C. H. Spurgeon* [S7]:

**A child and an apple:** To accept Christ in faith is a quite simple process. Let us imagine a child is supposed to get an apple from his father. He holds the apple out and promises to give it to the child, if he comes and gets it. With this example, we illustrate trust and acceptance with a mere apple, but it is similar to faith, which deals with eternal salvation. The child's hand extending out to the apple represents full salvation in Christ through faith. The hand of the child does not produce the apple, does not improve it, does not earn it, it merely takes it. With faith it is similar. Whoever has faith accepts salvation in humbleness without attempting to earn it or cause it to happen. God chose faith as a tool, since this binds man with God. If we trust God, a relationship arises between God and us, which brings blessings with it. Faith saves us, because it causes us to cling to God and stay in contact with him. This can be illustrated by an event which occurred many years ago:

Above the **Niagara Falls** a boat capsized. Both passengers were dragged towards the rushing waterfall. Some people on the bank managed to throw a rope to the shipwrecked men. *One* of these grabbed on the rope and was pulled to safety on land. The *other,* however, saw a large tree trunk floating by. He let the rope go by and clung onto the tree trunk, since this seemed more reliable to him due to its size. The tree trunk with the man was dragged over the edge. There was no connection between the one seeking help and the shore where safety lay. The size of the tree trunk alone did not provide salvation. That is how it will also be with people who trust in their own works, own philosophy of life, or in the great religions for their salvation, since there is no connection with Christ. The first ship-wrecked man grabbed the thin, insignificant-looking rope and was rescued from a certain death. In this manner, faith, though it may appear to us to be only a thin rope, is sufficient to bring us over to the other shore, since it lies in the hands of the great God. The rope tossed to us through Christ, which we must grab onto, makes us righteous and saves us from eternal damnation. Only this righteousness is acceptable to God, since it is based on God's own righteousness.

The letter of Hebrews states that faith is a necessary pre-requisite to pleasing God: "And without faith it is impossible to please God, because anyone who comes to him must believe that he exists" (Hebr 11:6). What kind of faith is meant here? We must distinguish between different kinds of belief.

## 8.1 Types of Belief

**1. Superstition:** We were warned already in the Old Testament about this "form of belief", which the Lord hates: "Let no-one be found among you ... who practises divination or sorcery, interprets omens, engages in witchcraft, or casts spells, or who is a medium or spiritist or who consults the dead. Anyone who does these things is detestable to the Lord" (Deut 18:10-12). The radio evangelist *Richard Kriese* has warned us in his book, "The Attack of Occultism", about these practices and unmasked them as works of demons [K4]: "Superstition in all its manifestations is often made fun of and yet wide-spread: It is apparently developing a new offensive using combined systems of attack by demonic powers ... unlucky numbers and lucky numbers, bad luck signs and good luck signs are taken much more seriously than most people suspect. People pay attention to black cats and chimney sweeps and have nothing against amulets." Talisman, horoscopes, cards, pendulums, and so on, are expressions of superstition, which being false doctrine, lead us astray.

**2. Idolatry:** The Bible expresses in numerous places the invalidity of belief in heathen idols and discusses its existence among God's people. In Isaiah 44:9-20 we find a thorough description of the characteristics and evaluation of the worship of idols:

> "All who make idols are nothing, and the things they treasure are worthless. Those who would speak up for them are blind; they are ignorant, to their own shame. Who shapes a god and casts an idol, which can profit him nothing? He and his kind will be put to shame; craftsmen are nothing but men. Let them all come together and take their stand; they will be brought down to terror and infamy.

> The **blacksmith** takes a tool and works with it in the coals; he shapes an idol with hammers, he forges it with the might of his arm. He gets hungry and loses his strength; he drinks no water and grows faint.

> The **carpenter** measures with a line and makes an outline with a marker; he roughs it out with chisels and marks it with compasses. He shapes it in the form of man, of man in all his glory, that it may dwell in a shrine. He cut down cedars, or perhaps took a cypress or oak. He let it grow among the trees of the forest, or planted a pine, and the rain made it grow. It is man's fuel for burning; **some of it** he takes and warms himself, he kindles a fire and bakes bread. But he also fashions a god and worships it; he makes an idol and bows down to it. Half of the wood he burns in the fire; over it he prepares his meal, he roasts his meat and eats his fill. He also warms himself and says, 'Ah! I am warm; I see the fire.'

> From **the rest** he makes a god, his idol; he bows down to it

and worships. He prays to it and says, 'Save me; you are my god.'

They know nothing, they understand nothing; their eyes are plastered over so they cannot see, and their minds closed so they cannot understand. No-one stops to think, no-one has the knowledge or understanding to say, 'Half of it I used for fuel; I even baked bread over its coals, I roasted meat and I ate. Shall I make a detestable thing from what is left? Shall I bow down to a block of wood?' He feeds on ashes, a deluded heart misleads him; he cannot save himself, or say, 'Is not this thing in my right hand a lie?' "

The judgment of God on all humanly invented cults reads: "These gods, who did not make the heavens and the earth, will perish from the earth ... and they have no breath in them. They are worthless, the objects of mockery; when their judgment comes, they will perish" (Jer 10:11-15). Salvation is not to be found here. As already indicated, every belief in the various religions can be put into this category. The idols are by no means always made out of wood, stone, or metal; invisible gods are frequently worshipped (for example, in Hinduism and Islam, but also in the so-called Christian countries in the form of pantheism, theism, deism or anthroposophy).

**3. Belief in probability:** You meet someone and ask: "Is your brother home?" He says: "I believe so." Your response to "Don't you know whether your brother is there?" is the answer: "I am not certain, but I believe so." In everyday conversation we often use the word "believe" as an expression of uncertainty. In this sense, one is speaking of a generally accepted belief. One could express ones uncertainty better with, "I don't know exactly", or, "I assume", instead of "believe"; otherwise "believe" is robbed of its own true meaning. The Biblical concept of "belief" (Greek *pisteuein* = to be faithful, to believe, to trust) means something which is stable, certain, sure, and which is founded on trust, even though the object of the belief is not visible: "Now faith is being sure of what we hope for and certain of what we do not see" (Hebr 11:1).

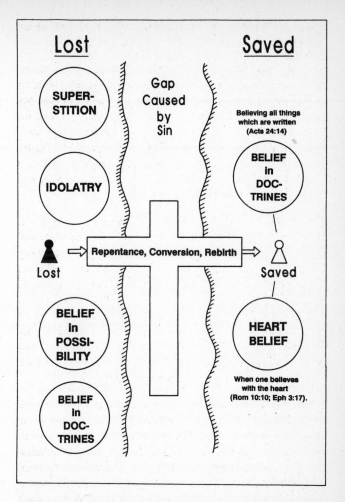

**Figure 15:** *Types of belief on the side of those lost and the saving belief made possible through the cross of Jesus Christ through repentance, conversion and being born again.*

**4. Belief in doctrines:** Blind acceptance of doctrinal statements is risky. Opinions and teachings of a church are generally accepted as true. One accepts a doctrinal statement of faith and even has a great knowledge of the Bible, which is appreciated and certainly not to be criticised. This belief in doctrine alone is, however, not stable and cannot save. *Luther* recognised this. He called the mere acceptance of doctrines and stories "historical faith". He said such belief does not help at all, "It is merely works without grace, and even the damned have as much."

The devil knows the Bible well. During Jesus' temptation (Matt 4:1-11) he demonstrated his knowledge of the Bible. The New Testament witnesses that the devil also has a belief in the Biblical doctrine: "You believe that there is one God. Good! Even the demons believe that-and shudder" (James 2:19). In spite of this knowledge that Jesus is God's son (Matt 4:3+6), the devil has already been judged (John 16:11).

**5. Believing with the heart in Jesus:** If knowledge and belief in Biblical claims (doctrinal belief) comes together with a personal relationship with Jesus Christ (heart belief), then we have a saving belief: "For it is with your heart that you believe and are justified, and it is with your mouth that you confess and are saved. As the Scripture says, 'Everyone who trusts in him will never be put to shame' ... the same Lord is Lord of all and richly blesses all who call on him, for, 'Everyone who calls on the name of the Lord will be saved.'" (Rom 10:10-13). Such belief means total faith in Jesus Christ. Jesus uses the Roman captain from Capernaum as an example, since the captain trusted in Him entirely (Matt 8:5-13). Saving faith means surrendering one's own will in complete trust. It gives God the honour, since it recognises God's standards and causes one to turn to him in repentance and conversion. The saving faith in Jesus is not just some concept about him, but thoroughly founded on the Scripture: "Whoever believes in me, as the Scripture has said, streams of living water will flow from within him" (John 7:38). Whoever says YES to the statements of the Holy Scriptures and accepts Jesus in faith *is* saved. We wish to demonstrate using various central Biblical verses that salvation comes through believing with the heart in Jesus:

| | |
|---|---|
| Mark 16:16: | "**Whoever believes** and is baptised will be saved, but whoever does not believe will be condemned." |
| John 5:24: | "Whoever hears my word and **believes** him who sent me, has eternal life and will not be condemned; he has crossed over from death to life." |
| John 3:16: | "... that **whosoever believes** in him shall not perish but have eternal life." |
| John 11:25-26: | "**He who believes in me**, will live, even though he dies; and whoever lives and believes in me will never die." |
| John 20:31: | "But these (signs) are written, **that you may believe** that Jesus is the Christ, the Son of God, and that by believing you may have life in his name." |
| Acts 13:39: | "Through him **everyone who believes** is justified from all everything." |
| Acts 16:31: | "**Believe in the Lord Jesus Christ**, and you will be saved." |
| Rom. 3:22: | "This righteousness from God comes **through faith in Jesus Christ** to all who believe." |
| Rom 3:26: | "... so as to be just and the one who justifies the man **who has faith in Jesus**." |
| 1 John 5:12: | "He who has the Son has life; he who does not have the Son of God does not have life." |

These Bible verses clearly state that we are not saved:

- by believing what most people believe
- by believing in something specific
- by believing something earnestly

but rather:

- by believing in Jesus (**who**)
- by believing what the Scriptures say about Jesus (**what**)
- by believing with the whole heart in Jesus (**how**)

## 8.2 The Foundation of Faith: Jesus Christ

Even as every building needs a solid foundation, God has established Jesus Christ as the foundation of our faith: "God presented him (Jesus) as a sacrifice of atonement, through faith in his blood" (Rom 3:25). Since this is the only way leading to salvation, *Paul* wrote, "For no-one can lay any foundation other than the one already laid, which is Jesus Christ" (1 Cor 3:11). Faith placed in Christ is not based on human wisdom, but on God's power (Rom 1:16; 1 Cor 2:5). This faith is neither a matter of human works nor human achievement, but the gift of God. The call to faith is always both a message from the Word of God (Rom 10:17) and a witness about Jesus Christ: "He (Jesus) commanded us to preach to the people and to testify that he is the one whom God appointed as judge of the living and the dead. All the prophets testify about him that everyone who believes in him receives forgiveness of sins through his name" (Acts 10:42-43).

Jesus was unique in the history of the world:
- He himself never wrote anything; nevertheless, his words in the Gospel have been translated into more languages than any other written documents in the history of the world
- Over 60,000 biographies have been written about him
- No other person has been displayed so often in paintings
- The New Testament reports about over 37 miracles which he performed
- Of all places Jesus went to, only one itinerary is known exactly: his last trip to Jerusalem. It was the way to the cross!

## 8.3 Stages of Faith: the Fulfilled Life

Faith is not static, a closed matter after repentance and conversion; it must remain dynamic and lively one's whole life long. Some stages of faith will be outlined next.

**1. Faith grows**: It is always a miracle when a person turns to the Lord Jesus with his whole heart and is thus saved for all eternity. Yet it is false when that person thinks, "Now I am saved! Everything is okay! I've made it! Let's leave it at that!" That would be totally unbiblical. Once we have accepted the Lord Jesus through his grace, we are like newborn babies. The one who has just been born again, irrespective of his natural age, is a baby in faith and must grow. *C. S. Lewis* (1898-1963) compared this to an egg [L3, 43]: "For an egg it may appear to be a small matter to change into a bird, but it would certainly be a more difficult matter to learn how to fly and still remain an egg." The apostle *Peter* admonished, "But grow in the grace and knowledge of our Lord and Saviour Jesus Christ" (2 Peter 3:18). Faith should cause one to develop "until we all reach unity in the faith and in the knowledge of the Son of God and become mature, attaining to the whole measure of the fullness of Christ" (Eph 4:13), so that we stand firm in faith and life. The new child of God requires proper food: "Like newborn babies, crave pure spiritual milk, so that by it you may grow up in your salvation" (1 Peter 2:2). But those mature in faith also need nourishment: "But solid food is for the mature, who by constant use have trained themselves to distinguish good from evil" (Hebr 5:14). Both "milk" and "solid food" are found in the Bible. Whoever wishes to grow in faith, as God has commanded, must read the Bible. Whoever does so, will be richly blessed. Some testimonies about the Bible should help us. The German reformer *Martin Luther* (1483-1546) said: "The Bible is not antiquated, also not modern, it is eternal." The German author *Manfred Hausmann* (1898-1986) wrote: "The Word of God was indeed written by men, but not thought up by men. One calls it the book of books. In it one finds a true description of man, written clearly and rationally; one reads about his glory and pitifulness, his magnanimity and misery, his dreams and burdens. Because it does not idealise man, but looks at man realistically and truthfully, the Bible and the message contained in it deserves to be trusted." In addition to reading the Bible, prayer and fellowship with other believers promote healthy growth in faith.

**2. Faith is obedient**: Our love for Jesus is displayed in obedience to him. Obedience is the visible fruit of faith. The Bible says to us: "We must obey God rather than men" (Acts 5:29). This obedience frees us from all human fear and leads us to the "glorious freedom of the child of God." Faith and obedience are coupled so tightly together, that the Lord Jesus even described obedience as a prerequisite to gaining insight into Biblical teachings: "My teaching is not my own. It comes from him who sent me. If anyone chooses to do God's will, he will find out whether my teaching comes from God or whether I speak on my own" (John 7:16-17). Whoever is not prepared to be obedient cannot experience faith. Thus *Dietrich Bonhoeffer* (1906-1945) could say, "Only the obedient believe, and only believers obey." If we say we love God but do not obey his commandments and trust his word, our being is a living lie. God tests our love and our faith on the basis of his Word: "This is love for God: to obey his commands. And his commands are not burdensome (1 John 5:3). The appearance of "theistical evolution" [G2] can thus be viewed as disobedience towards the Word of God.

**3. Faith endures temptation and struggle**: The believer finds himself in this world in enemy territory. The things which surround us, thoughts and actions, are for the most part, shaped through disbelief; "the faithful have vanished from among men" (Ps 12:1). Faith must be preserved despite temptation: "Be self-controlled and alert. Your enemy the devil prowls around like a roaring lion looking for someone to devour. Resist him, standing firm in the faith" (1 Peter 5:8-9). Temptation itself is not a sin. Whoever endures temptation and overcomes it will be blessed (James 1:12).

Since my childhood, I am particularly fond of sunflowers. One year, after planting sunflower seeds in several places in our garden, a kind of parable occurred to me about the growing plants. Some grew quite near the house, under a roof, protected from the wind. These grew very rapidly and reached a height of 3 meters with their thin reeds. Others stood in the open, were soon "attacked" by the wind and developed an appropriately strong stem and roots. One day a storm came and broke or knocked over the stems of the well-protected sunflowers near the house, while the sunflowers standing in the open easily survived the storm, because they were accustomed to challenge. In the same way, tested faith will stand fast against tribulations and temptations.

We can ward off the "flaming arrows of the evil one" (Eph 6:16) illustrated in *Figure 16* with the shield of faith, so that they are ineffective. *Paul* advised us to "fight the good fight of the faith" (1 Tim 6:12). Those belonging to different ideologies fight among themselves about beliefs. The fight of faith is different. It occurs as a witness and service to this world.

During an evangelisation in Brunswick (a German town between Hanover and Berlin where the author lives) with *Richard Kriese,* a group of believers marched through the inner city. This march of witnesses, which consisted of about 300 believers, ended at the castle courtyard in front of the Brunswick cathedral. When we arrived at the courtyard, two groups of demonstrators from the German National Socialist Party (NPD) and from communist parties had squared off against each other. A fight between these two groups with conflicting ideologies could only be prevented by a large police contingent, who built a chain with their protective shields. The exchange of shouts and jeering whistles was a vivid demonstration of hate. On the cathedral side of the yard, the believers formed a large choir. Many songs of salvation were sung, about the love of God and the power of Jesus' forgiveness. It was clear to us: in the battle of faith, we should pay witness to the Gospel and offer this to a lost world.

**4. Faith brings victory**: When we speak about victory, we must first name the victor: it is Jesus Christ! His words on the cross, "It is fulfilled!" fundamentally changed the situation of the world. The powers of darkness have been defeated. Since Jesus' resurrection, "Death has been swallowed up in victory" (1 Cor 15:54) and "By his death he might destroy him who holds the power of death, that is, the devil" (Hebr 2:14). From that day on, the death of Jesus was the death of death itself. The resurrection of Jesus from death is the seal of victory. Why? An event from European history helps to explain this:

In the year 1815 the allies in the Belle Alliance triumphed against *Napoleon*, who had ruled over practically all of Europe. In a private letter, field marshal *A. N. von Gneisenau* (1760-1831) wrote about the victory. On the envelope of the letter he wrote, "Please notice the seal!" This seal was, you see, stamped with *Napoleon's* seal, which someone had found on the evening of the battle in his captured wagon. So the loser *Napoleon* had to confirm his own downfall with his own seal.

Death was the seal of the powers of darkness, a symbol of power, a seal of the devil. Through Jesus' death and his unique resurrection the enemy has been overcome. Jesus has the sign of power; he has the keys to hell and death. Our faith is linked with Jesus' victory. Our faith is so closely coupled with Jesus' resurrection, that *Paul* said, "If Christ has not been raised, our preaching is useless (1 Cor 15:14). However, he did rise from the dead and our faith lies on the victor's side. Someone once said, "When we are healthy in our faith, then we are invincible." This confidence in victory, not founded on ourselves but on the relationship to the son of God, was emphasised by the apostle *John*: "This is the victory that has overcome the world, even our faith" (1 John 5:4).

# 9 How Does the Gospel Differ from Other Ways?

## 9.1 How Does the Gospel Differ from Religions?

Some marked differences between religions and the Gospel from a Biblical point of view are summarised below [G3, 84-85]:

**1.** In all religions man seeks on his own to reach God, but none of these people seeking God can honestly claim, "I have found a personal relationship with God, I have peace in my heart, my guilt is forgiven, I have the certainty of eternal life." In the Gospel of Jesus Christ, however, God comes to us. With the cross, he bridges the gap caused by sin and gives us redemption. Whoever accepts this can testify that, "For I am convinced that neither death nor life ... will be able to separate us from the love of God" (Rom 8:38-39).

**2.** The Prophecies of a saviour in the Old Testament (OT) (Gen 3:15; Num 24:17; Isaiah 11:1-2; Isaiah 7:14) were literally fulfilled. In no religion are there such prophecies which were announced and fulfilled.

**3.** God has judged all religions as idolatry and sorcery (1 Cor 6:9-10; Gal 5:19-21; Rev 21:8). Whoever practices one will be judged by God: "A deluded heart misleads him; he cannot save himself" (Isaiah 44:20). Only Jesus has been authorised by God to be our saviour: "This is my Son, whom I love; with him I am well pleased. Listen to him" (Matt 17:5). At Jesus' birth, the angel announced, "Today ... a Saviour has been born to you" (Luke 2:11).

**4.** God authenticated Jesus Christ's sacrifice through Christ's resurrection from the dead (Rom 4:24-25). Jesus was the only person who left his grave alive, never to die again: "Why do you look for the living among the dead? He is not here, he has risen!" (Luke 24:5-6). All founders of religions have died and remain dead.

**5.** In all religions man attempts to redeem himself through his own efforts. The Gospel, on the other hand, is an act of God. Man cannot contribute to the redemptive work at Golgotha: we have been purchased for a great price (1 Cor 6:20). Religion has the same relationship with the Gospel, as man's acts have with respect to God's acts.

**6.** In no religion does God leave heaven to save man. Through Jesus, God became a man: "The Word became flesh, and lived for a while among us. (We have seen his glory, the glory of the one and only Son, who came from the Father), full of grace and truth" (John 1:14).

**7.** Religions prevent us from attaining God's kingdom (Rev 21:8), but the Gospel allows believers to enter God's Kingdom "because it is the power of God for the salvation" (Rom 1:16).

## 9.2  The Features and Consequences of Sects

In this sub-chapter, I primarily want to look at religious movements which have digressed from Christianity. The non-Christian movements (e.g. Divine Light Mission, the Unification Church of San Myung Mun, Scientology, Bahai) have been dealt with under the section Religion in definition D1 (see chapter 4.2) and they have already been assessed in the light of the Bible. The founders of the sects we are dealing with came from a Christian background. However they then developed a special teaching and laid such emphasis on it that these groups can no longer be referred to as Christian.

### 9.2.1  Definition of a Sect

The word **sect** is derived either from the late Latin word *secta* (a different way of thinking or behaviour) or from *secare* (cut, remove). *Secare* is the etymological root of dissect (to open a corpse, to take apart), as well as *section* and *sector*. Another theory is that the word derives from the word *sequor* (to follow, in the sense of following a sect) and this is equally apt. The Jewish-Greek philosopher, *Philo of Alexandria* (circa 25 BC - 50 AD) and the Jewish historian, *Flavius Josephus* (37/38 - 100 AD) refer to the Pharisees, the Saducees, the Essenes and the Greek philosophical schools as secta. The word describes a school, party or school of thought and suggests something private and unauthorised. In the NT we find the parallel term heresy (Greek *haíresis*), as in 1 Cor 11:19; Gal 5:20; 1 Peter 2:1, for example. The followers or members of the *heiresis* are heretics (Greek, *hairetikós*) which means someone who makes a free decision in favour of a school of thought or party.

**Sectarians** are those who follow a false doctrine, which has become isolated from the message of the Gospel. They follow their own special teaching. The Bible warns against sects because they lead people astray in the same way as other religions do. The appearance of sects is nothing new. They have been forging the saving Gospel since the days of the early church:

> "But there were also false prophets among the people, just as there will be false teachers among you. They will secretly introduce destructive heresies, even denying the sovereign Lord who bought them (*i. e. denying that he is the only Saviour and Redeemer, and the only way to the Father in Heaven*) – bringing swift destruction on themselves" (2 Peter 2:1).

### 9.2.2 The Breeding Ground for Sects

Many, especially young people, have rejected today's **society**. **Politicians** offer no satisfactory answers to their questions. Nowadays **Science** creates more problems than it solves. Materialistic philosophies of life have turned man into a soulless being and destroyed his identity. The future with its unavoidable problems (like the crises of the environment, of energy, economics, ethics) is worrying and seems hopeless.

Security is found more and more seldom in **families** and the **church** is losing ground and influence, their empty message being the result of liberal theology.

People are looking for advice and help. And this is where the sects come in. The collapse of communism in the now liberated former East Block countries has caused a spiritual vacuum and the sects are taking great advantage of this. Their **ready made End Time Doctrine** addresses the future and thus meets the needs of many who are afraid of the what the future may hold. Their strictly organised communities offer a certain security.

### 9.2.3 How to Identify a Sect

Some general features of sects are mentioned briefly in eight points below:

**1. Only a section of the Bible is taught:** The sects only teach a part, a section of the Bible – rather like one piece of cake out of a whole. This part is true because it is taken from the Bible. The section taken from the Bible is of different lengths and is chosen according to different criteria, depending on the type of sect involved. This small piece of truth is then mixed up with the special false teaching of that particular sect.

**2. The central truth of the Gospel is missing:** According to the teaching of the NT, we need to be converted to Jesus Christ in order to be saved. This personal faith in the Son of God is absolutely necessary for salvation – thus it is the central truth in the doctrine of salvation. If it is necessary to turn to Jesus in order to get to heaven, if Jesus is the only way to the Father then not to teach this is to deprive people of the most important thing in life. (NB. If this central truth of the Gospel is missing in established churches then they stray into the area of the sects.)

**3. False teaching about Jesus Christ:** The sects forge the biblical teaching about Jesus Christ, the Son of God and the only Redeemer. Each sect alters the teaching in a different way. For the *Christian Scientists*, Jesus is not God, he is simply "the name of a person who embodied God's idea of divinity more than anyone else". The *Jehovah's Witnesses* teach that Jesus was created by God. In heaven Jesus was the archangel Michael. On earth he was a human being, but not God. God raised him from the dead and he returned to heaven as a spirit.

**4. The founder's revelations or doctrines are set against the Bible:** As someone with a knowledge of the Bible, the false teachings of the sects are relatively easy to recognise and disprove. Even the members of the sect could do so, as they possess Bibles. The Bible is a complete work, from which nothing can be taken away and to which nothing can be added (Rev 22:18-19). This statement is a problem for all the sects. Their solution goes as follows: We've got a new revelation – at least, that is what the founders of the sects claim – , which is not just equally authoritative but of a far higher authority than the Bible. They go one step further than the Bible: they change its message, either adding or subtracting some aspect.

The *Mormons* say that the Bible is imperfect and so their "Book of Mormon" is more important. *Mary Baker Eddy*, the founder of *Christian Science* authorises her work as follows, "I would be ashamed to write it if it was of human origin, if I, without God, were its author. But I am only the scribe who passes on the heavenly harmonies of the divine doctrine of nature." In the *New Apostolic Church* the highest authority is what their own apostles says – it has a higher authority than the Bible.

**5. Possibility of Salvation after death:** Jesus taught the truth about heaven and hell, he talked about salvation and the lost (e. g. Matt 7:13-14; Matt 18:8-9; Matt 25:21,30; Matt 25:46; John 3:16; John 3:36), he preached eternal life (John 10:27-29; John 11:25) and warned about being lost for ever (Matt 18:8-9). The epistle to the Hebrews says that everything is decided at death, "Just as man is destined to die once and after that to face judgment" (Hebrews 9:27). The sects accommodate the wishes of a lot of people by omitting this biblical teaching and offering a way of salvation after death. They maintain that their particular sect is the only one for which this is possible. A lot of people have difficulties when they begin to consult the Bible on this point. What will happen to family and friends who seemingly die as unbelievers? And this is where the sects come in with their false teaching and give the impression of offering a solution to the problem. Thus among the *Mormons* one can be baptised on behalf of the dead and so save these deceased unbelievers long after their death. The *New Apostolic Church* offers socalled "sealing" which can be widened to include a dead person if it is carried out on a living person on their behalf.

**6. Exclusiveness and a claim to sole representation:** One striking feature of sects is their claim that salvation can be found solely in their community (and not in Jesus).

*Jehovah's Witnesses:* The death of Christ on the cross – or on the stake, as they like to call it – does not bring eternal life. Jesus' death can be seen as a sacrifice which buys us free from past sins but the only guarantee of salvation is constant effort to obey God in the way taught by the Watchtower Society. *Mormons:* They believe that they will be the only ones to enter heaven. They can be baptised on behalf of deceased ancestors so that they can become Mormons posthumously and so reach heaven.

Strict organisation is necessary to ensure exclusiveness, a claim to sole representation and solidarity. Thus a strong awareness of authority is evident in the sects. A tight hierarchical organisation with the corresponding powers is evident from the top leadership down to the local groups.

**7. People are led astray in the sects:** In the sects we see one of Satan's methods of temptation. People who are caught up in these sects are no longer free. They are bound in Satan's trap (2 Tim 2:26). It is extremely rare that someone manages to escape from it. In a very broad spectrum the devil offers exactly what appeals to people in their individual situation:

- for those who are scientifically orientated there is anthroposophy

- for those who are ill there is Christian Science which teaches that illness is all in the mind
- for those who are discontented with the church there are the Jehovah's Witnesses

In a fallen world we should not be surprised at the appearance of sects. For this reason the NT has many warnings about false teachers and prophets:

**Jesus**: "Watch out for false prophets. They come to you in sheep's clothing, but inwardly they are ferocious wolves" (Matt 7:15).

**Jesus**: "Watch out that no-one deceives you" (Matt 24:4).

**Paul**: "If anyone is preaching to you a gospel other than what you accepted, let him be eternally condemned" (Gal 1:9).

**Paul**: "Let no-one deceive you" (Eph 5:6).

**John**: "Many deceivers ... have gone out into the world ... Watch out that you do not lose what you have worked for ... Anyone who runs ahead and does not continue in the teaching of Christ does not have God" (2 John 7-9).

**8. People in a sect**: People in a sect are usually friendly even if they are somewhat pushy. Their enthusiasm for mission knows no bounds. Unfortunately their aim is not to preach salvation through Jesus Christ but to spread their special doctrines and win people for their particular community. The members of a sect are not any worse than anyone else, just as non-Christians are not necessarily any worse than Christians (The important thing is that Christians have a Saviour. Their sins are forgiven and they have eternal life through Christ).

The motives of these special communities are not dishonour-able. Sect members often surpass Christians with regards to their courage in bearing witness, their willingness in sacrifice and in persecution and in the way they apply what they believe to their lives. The witness of their faith and life is often very impressive. Living in such a community can seem fascinating and attractive to outsiders. But all these things should not hide the fact that they are false teaching which twists God's Word (Jer 23:36).

### 9.2.4  Consequences of the Sects and our Assessment

There are only two ways to bring about someone's physical death, other than using violence: we either deprive the body of its needs (e. g. food, drink, oxygen) or poison it.

It is the same in the spiritual world. A person dies spiritually if he is deprived of the necessary truth or if he is poisoned by false teaching. Both these things are the results of the sects. In the sects the biblical way of salvation is omitted and, just as in other religions, a way of saving one's own soul is offered.[1]

At this point I want to mention the most well-known sects by name: Jehovah's Witnesses, Mormons, Christian Scientists, Anthroposophy.

As Christians, how should we behave toward sect members? We find an answer to this question in the letter of Jude:

" ... snatch others from the fire and save them!" (Jude 23).

I would like to clarify here that the numerous evangelical churches are not sects, for example, Baptists, Brethren, Free Evangelical Churches, Salvation Army, Methodists, City Missions. In these churches Jesus is preached as the only Saviour and they do not claim to be the only group to enter heaven.

---

[1] In this assessment of the sects, the author does not wish to condemn all sect members. God can save individuals from these communities. Only the Lord knows how many and who will be saved. The point of this chapter is rather to warn people of the danger which these sects represent and which is clearly laid out in the Bible.

# 10 Man without the Gospel: Saved or Lost?

The previous chapters have shown that salvation through the Gospel occurs for those who accept it. The situation for those who do not accept it is unambiguous, since the Word of God is like a sword, which makes a sharp cut dividing the saved from the lost. A serious question that still remains: what about those who have never heard the Gospel and have gone the route of some religion? (See definition D1 in chapter 4.2).

If there is to be some hope for the heathen, then statements in the Bible must be found, since "the Sovereign Lord does nothing without revealing his plan" (Amos 3:7). We have found that there are many teachings about salvation which are not based on the Bible and do not follow the path described thoroughly in chapters 5 through 8. We would be pleased if God had revealed other possibilities, since we could in this manner comfort many others and feel less of a burden for the mission we have not fulfilled. Therefore one must test those possibilities which one occasionally encounters to distinguish between those based on the Bible and those developed by man, which are mere speculation.

## 10.1 Preaching to the Dead: A Second Chance?

There is a widely held view that after death, the Gospel can still be preached, giving those people the opportunity to make a decision, who either did not make the decision or rejected Christ during their lives. It has been reported that pastor *Johann Christoph Blumhardt* (1805-1880) preached to the dead, while in his dressing room at his church.

Two passages in the New Testament are given as references for this doctrine: Eph 4:8-10 and 1 Peter 3:18-20. It would go beyond the intentions of this book to deal in depth with these difficult passages. Interested readers are referred to the Appendix. At this point we will, however, mention the fundamental statement from Hebrews 9:27: "Just as man is destined to die once, and after that to face judgment." The Bible does not speak anywhere about the preaching the Gospel to the dead.

## 10.2  The All-Will-Be-Saved Doctrine: Salvation without Exception?

The all-will-be-saved doctrine claims that in the end all men will be saved. While Jesus said that the wide path leads to perdition, the all-will-be-saved doctrine claims that all human ways lead to eternal life and all attitudes of rejection towards God in life will remain without lasting consequences. Jesus said about *Judas*: "It would be better for him if he had not been born" (Matt 26:24). Would the Lord have said that if *Judas* could actually look forward to an eternity in heaven? In a more exact translation the Lord said to the traitor: "It would be better for *him* if he had not been born, that man!" But the all-will-be-saved proponents translate here differently: "It would have been nice for Him (that is, Jesus!) if he had not been born, that man (that is, *Judas*)." Through a small change (capitalising the word "*Him*" ), the meaning reversed. In this way, it is claimed that Jesus made a statement, which fits into the existing system. The apostle John stated unambiguously: "Whoever believes in the Son has eternal life, but whoever rejects the Son will not see life, for God's wrath remains on him" (John 3:36). The Lord Jesus speaks again and again of two eternal places, in which He invites us to heaven (for example, Matt 7:13-14; Luke 13:24; Luke 14:16-24) and warns us seriously about the place of perdition (for example, Matt 5:29-30; Matt 7:21-23; Matt 10:28; Matt 18:8; Mark 9:47-48; Luke 16:19-31).

Representatives of the all-will-be-saved doctrine argue, with typically human thinking, that it is unfair to punish people forever though they "only" sinned in time. Here it is necessary to observe: no one can argue with God (Rom 9:20). Only God can inform us how serious sin is to him. The Bible teacher *René Pache* commented in this respect that, *"Adam's* fall in sin and the cross of Christ are both time-limited events, yet both have eternal effects"* [P1].

The changed meaning of the word eternity to a time-limited concept plays a central role in the interpretation of the all-will-be-saved doctrine. In the original New Testament text the adjective *"aion"* stands for *"eternal"* . Though there are places in the New Testament, where from contextual meaning a time-limited meaning is to be understood (for example, Luke 1:70: "... since the ages began" ), in general, unlimited time is to be understood. *René Pache* [P1] determined that the word *"eternal"* has been applied 64 times to heavenly realities (for example, the eternal God, the eternal kingdom, eternal life, eternal glory) and 7 times the word is found in context with perdition (for example, eternal fire, eternal suffering). In Matthew 25:46 the Lord Jesus used the same adjective to describe eternal life and for eternal suffering in order to emphasise the finality of both. The all-will-be-saved doctrine reduces the eternity of hell to a time-limited punishment, since it assumes in all such cases a time-limited "aion" concept. We would like to warn against trying to explain the Bible using preconceived doctrines.

The all-will-be-saved doctrine lures people into false security, leading them to believe they will all be saved, irrespective of belief. It releases Christians from their personal duty to witness and devalues the work of evangelists and missionaries, making their sacrifices seem superfluous. It removes the seriousness of the eternal fate of a person. The Bible tells us that the last judgment is final and irrevocable, it has an eternal character. It can be too late! God rejected Saul due to his disobedience (1 Sam 15:23). God did not modify this verdict even though Saul asked for forgiveness (1 Sam 15:24-26).

**Temptations:** *Figure 16* shows the tricks of the devil, the father of lies, the lie since the beginning, the opposer, who roams around "like a roaring lion looking for someone to devour" (1 Peter 5:8).

The basic method used to lead people astray, using "Did God really say?" (Gen 3:1) has not changed since the first sin, but the exact nature of the attack is adjusted for each individual. Jesus was also tempted by the Devil. With Jesus he attempted, among other things, to challenge his authority as the Son of God: "If you are the Son of God, then ..." (Matt 4:3+5). Jesus withstood all temptations since he used God's word as solid support: "It is written!" In a like manner, the Devil has special methods to tempt each person:

- the believers in pious and often ungodly ways, because he appeals to the natural flesh and religious nature of man
- the non-believers, to keep them on their lost way through distractions and temptations
- the heathen by strengthening their idolatry
- the atheist in their godlessness by supporting the relevant doctrines (for example, existentialism, nihilism, natural philosophies, evolution).

The Devil cannot take the Bible away from those who believe in the **Bible,** so he uses the tactic: the whole Bible is true, but the meaning of the words can be changed or turned around. This principle was already established by the time of the first sin. The Devil never quotes God correctly. God gave man authority over everything He created (Gen 1:28-30), including all trees in the garden of Eden (Gen 2:16). Only a single tree, that is, the tree of the knowledge of good and evil (Gen 2:17), was excluded. The Devil, however, twisted God's statement into a question: "You must not eat from any tree in the garden?" (Gen 3:1). The Devil is the Bible critic par excellence. It is especially important to be attentive to such influences. *Thomas Schirrmacher* emphasised [S5, 126]: "When Christians believe their attitude towards the Bible is not a question of salvation, then they completely overlook that their salvation is only found

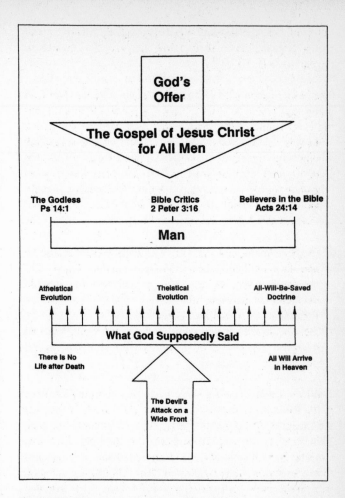

**Figure 16:** *The human situation in the gap between godlessness and Biblical faith. The saving Gospel is offered to all, and all find themselves confronted with the tempting question, "Did God really say?". Man has the freedom of decision.*

revealed in the Scriptures and that God's Word will be the judge of salvation or non-salvation! Bible criticism is like insult to royalty, and it is quite irrelevant whether it refers to a doubt, active opposition, or a pious method to extend the Bible or change its meaning. Bible criticism is not a peccadillo (slight offence)!"

The devil has taken the Bible partially or entirely away from the adherents of **Biblical criticism**. They trust in their own theories more than the Word of God. They entrust themselves with the task of correcting, criticising, demythologising and emptying the Word. They are disobedient to God's Word (1 Sam 15:23). *Theistical evolution* [G2], for example, a belief in which people look for their ancestors in the animal kingdom, belongs in this category. Death is no longer considered as the wage of sin, but rather as a necessary evolutionary factor which allows upward development. The "critical-historical" method, is seen as an appropriate vehicle to interpret the Bible. Central events reported in the Bible as historical facts, such as the fall into sin of the first people, *Jonah* in the stomach of the fish and the physical resurrection of Jesus are viewed as mythology.

The devil has decreased the value of the Bible for the **godless** to that of a meaningless book. At best they consider it as having a certain literary value, but they deny God's power. They accept, for example, the theories of evolutionary teaching and think they have thus answered all significant questions about their origins, about the meaning and purpose of the world, and about life. *Paul* said that the deceiver "Has blinded the minds of unbelievers, so that they cannot see the light of the gospel of the glory of Christ, who is the image of God" (2 Cor 4:4).

The devil offers countless religions to **heathens who have not yet heard the Gospel**. He leads them to believe in spirits and idolatry, so that they worship "demons, and idols of gold, silver, bronze, stone and wood – idols that cannot see or hear or walk" (Rev 9:20).

## 10.3 God's Grace: Unlimited Range?

There are many innocent people, who have either never heard about Jesus Christ at all or have only heard the Gospel in watered down or distorted form. Many ask the question, how can God condemn people who have effectively never heard the Gospel? No, they argue, the door cannot remain closed forever to those who have never heard His name. God's grace must extend beyond those areas which have already been reached by the Gospel.

*G. D. Ladds*, a missionary, provided the following answer [S1]: "No, we do not slam the door on the millions who never heard the name of Jesus ... We emphasise, however, that only the cross and resurrection can save us. We further emphasise that non-Christian religions lack all redeeming truth. Some people however, may have reached out towards God or longed for eternal life even though they have never heard the Good News. These people have mentally undergone a true purification of the spirit and they are considered by God as worthy of salvation through Jesus. But how many, we don't know.

This view clearly has a better foundation in the Scriptures than the all-will-be-saved doctrine mentioned previously. God's grace has an unlimited physical range (Ps 108:5), that is, we could be saved on a rocket to the moon or at a depth of 1000 m in an underground mine. But whoever rejects this grace (" trampled under foot" , Hebr 10:29-31) cannot benefit from it. God's saving grace was displayed in the person of Jesus (Titus 2:11) and in him the range of God's grace attained its absolute measure: "He who has the Son has life; he who does not have the Son of God does not have life" (1 John 5:12). We would make God a liar, should we modify this Biblical standard (1 John 5:10).

**We Conclude**: We can't and don't wish to set any limits to God's mercy. God's grace extends farther than we can imagine, but nevertheless not further than witnessed in the Scriptures, since God's Word is immutable both as a judge and in its grace.

## 10.4 Heathens on Judgment Day: Criteria for the Judgment

Heathens, who have never heard the message of the Bible have, as shown in *Figure 12,* three sources of knowledge: **Creation** (Rom 1:20), **Conscience** (Rom 2:15) and the **Knowledge of Eternity** (Eccl 3:11). Creation witnesses to them that a God exists, and conscience, the inner voice given by God, says: what is right, and what is wrong. If a person does something wrong, the conscience gives him feelings of guilt and judgment. *Don Richardson* proves in his book "Eternity in their Hearts" [R1] that various peoples of the earth know about life after death. God has thus not left the heathen without evidence (Acts 14:17). To act against the warning of the conscience is sin. Whoever sins persistently weakens the conscience more and more. That can lead to the point where the conscience is dead and no longer reacts. There are people who lie so habitually, that they themselves are not even aware of it.

Do the heathen live according to their conscience? The Roman poet *Q. H. F. Horaz* (65-8 BC) stated: "I see a better way, but I follow the worse." The well-known missionary to China, *Hudson Taylor* (1832-1905), concluded after life-long experience with the heathen in China, that he never met a Chinese person who claimed to have lived totally according to the knowledge he had. Paul describes this situation in Romans 3:

- All are among the sinners
- No one is righteous
- No one understands
- No one seeks God
- They have all gone astray
- They have all become lazy
- No one does good works
- No one fears God.

Heathens, like all other people, do not always act according to their consciences. The knowledge of a creator and the existence of conscience makes people responsible for their actions. We would like to look more closely at the standards revealed in the Scriptures, by which God will judge us. The highest principle is, "It is unthinkable that God would do wrong, that the Almighty would pervert justice" (Job 34:12).

**According to the extent of revelation**: It is clear that non-evangelised heathens carry less responsibility than those people to whom the light of the Gospel has been revealed. Those, however, who hear the message have another status when they stand before God: they have been given the opportunity to be saved. If they didn't accept it, their judgment will be much more severe. The Lord said in Luke 12:48, "From everyone who has been given much, much will be demanded; and from the one who has been entrusted with much, much more will be asked." Jesus spoke, therefore, of various degrees of judgment. *Paul* distinguishes between those who "under the Law" sinned, and those who did so "without the Law." Because God judges without regard to the popularity or respectability of a person, he will surely take ones circumstances into consideration before judging.

**According to works**: God knows the actions of everyone and "Will give to each person according to what he has done" (Rom 2:6). Works are both the action one has carried out (Matt 25:34-40) and also those omitted (Matt 25:41-46). Man's actions are recorded in God's record books and form the basis for the judgment of unbelievers in God's court (Rev 20:12-13).

**Without respect to person**: People judge each other according to various criteria: where we come from, our education, clothing, prestige, titles and honours, possessions, popularity, nationality, even membership in a church. All these value criteria do not exist with God. The key with him is the principle, "*Without respect to the person!*" (1 Peter 1:17; Rom 2:11; Acts 10:34).

**In justice**: The Lord is a righteous judge (2 Tim 4:8). In Revelations 16:7, we read, "Yes, Lord God Almighty, true and just are your judgments."

In so many daily situations are people are divided into two groups. A small list should make us aware of this:

| on the train: | smokers and non-smokers |
|---|---|
| in swimming pools: | swimmers and non-swimmers |
| sports: | winners and losers |
| employment: | employees and employers |
| medicine: | healthy and sick |
| human statistics | men and women |
| traffic police: | with and without driver's license |

In God's court there will also be a division of mankind into two groups, but according to other categories:

the good and the evil – with nothing in between
light and darkness – without twilight
the saved and the lost – without "half-saved"
children of God and children of the devil – without neutral children
those receiving and those not receiving grace – with nothing in between
inheritors of heaven and those lost in hell – without purgatory
righteous and unrighteous – without mediocre
blessed and cursed – without "half-blessed"

The Irish writer *C. S. Lewis* brought it all together in a formula [L3, 64]: "At the end there will be only two kinds of people: those who say to God, 'Your will be done', and those to whom God says at the end, 'Your will be done'." While the Bible describes merely two categories of eternal destination, there are various categories of saved and unsaved people:

**The Saved:** The Lord Jesus speaks about small and great in the Kingdom of Heaven (Matt 5:19). Some are indeed saved, but "only as one escaping through the flames" (1 Cor 3:15), since their life has remained empty and fruitless for God despite being saved, and their lives with their vanity and facades ("wood, hay and straw") cannot stand before the fire of judgment: worthless for eternity, for God. The others, however, "Those who are wise will shine like the brightness of the heavens, and those who lead many to righteousness, like the stars for ever and ever" (Daniel 12:3). Each will be rewarded

116

according to his work (1 Cor 3:8; 1 Cor 3:14; Rev 2:10; Rev 3:21; and so on). This aspect is clearly expressed in the parable of the servants entrusted with money (Luke 19:11-28), who were later awarded according to what they had earned by investing the money. Whereas the "glory" in the Kingdom of God will differ in degrees, the "blessedness" (salvation) will be the same for all who are saved. This last concept was taught to us by the Lord in the parable of the workers in the vineyard (Matt 20:1-15), who all received the same wages, regardless of the length of their work-day.

**Lost:** There are also various levels of being non-saved. The Lord Jesus proved himself in special ways to be the Son of God in the cities of Chorazin and Bethsaida, but the people did not repent. Then he preached to them about the judgment. In comparison to other people who have not heard the call to repentance, they can expect a harsher punishment: "If the miracles that were performed in you had been performed in Tyre and Sidon, they would have repented long ago in sackcloth and ashes. But I tell you, it will be more bearable for Tyre and Sidon on the day of judgment than for you" (Matt 11:21-22). The citizens of Sodom will also be judged differently than those of Capernaum. Self-righteous and hypocritical scholars can expect especially severe punishment (Matt 23:13-33). The judgment of mass murders will be different than of "ordinary" citizens, who were indifferent about Jesus. People, who have heard the Gospel, but have not accepted it, are in a different position than heathens, who have never heard it.

## 10.5  If Heathens Are Lost: For What Reason?

Whoever hears the Gospel and is not converted remains lost. He remains in the fundamental situation in which *all men* (the natural man) find themselves:

- "Dead in your transgressions and sins, children of wrath from nature, without hope and without God" (Eph 2:1,3,12)
- Under "the power of Satan" (Acts 26:18)

- Living in darkness (Acts 26:18)
- Without forgiveness (Acts 26:18)
- "Without inheritance" (Eph 5:5)
- "Whoever believes in him is not condemned" (John 3:18).

We cannot ignore these questions when it comes to the issue of non-evangelised heathens. Are heathens lost,

- because they were born in the wrong country?
- because they never heard the Gospel?
- because they never had a chance to make a decision for Christ?
- because they did not accept a message which they never heard?

The answer is NO! *J. O. Sanders*, a missionary, gives an answer based on the bible [S1, 63]: "If heathens are lost, it is for the same reasons as other people: because they are sinners. All people, religious or civilised and those we call heathens, are lost, because they have sinned. All men were born with a sinful nature. 'For all have sinned, and come short of the glory of God' (Rom 3:23). A "natural man"[2], whether a heathen in a

---

[2] The New Testament divides people into three groups:

**1. psychikos** (Greek): This is a man controlled by his senses, that means, he is a sensuous, mental, *natural man*, which doesn't perceive anything about the spirit of God (James 3:15; 1 Cor 2:14). He lives with his worldly lusts, without God. He has not experienced being born again and has not been redeemed. By nature, all men from Adam on find themselves in this chain. The natural man can indeed be well-learned, friendly, polite, eloquent and helpful, but nevertheless the spiritual content of the Bible remains totally hidden from him.

**2. pneumatikos** (Greek): This is a natural man, made new by being born-again. He is a *spiritual man*, filled with the Holy Spirit and walks in close fellowship with God (Eph 5:18-20). He has been made a new creation "in Christ" , has eternal life (1 John 5:12), understands the spiritual dimension of the Bible (1 Cor 2:15-16) and hungers for the Word of God.

**3. sarkios** (Greek): This is a *flesh and blood man*, that is, a new man through the faith, who nevertheless "walks according to the flesh" (Gal 3:3). He remains a small child in Christ (1 Cor 3:1-4), who has only understood the simplest truths (" milk" ) (1 Cor 3:2).

remote jungle or in the middle of a highly technological world, does not seek the living God, his holiness and his light, since his attitude is: "Leave us alone! We have no desire to know your ways" (Job 21:14). In this manner man forms idols after his own image. As the well-known German poet *J. W. von Goethe* (1749-1832) described in "Prometheus" , he walks in the way of religion according to his own will and thoughts. The Bible describes this, "There is a way that seems right to a man, but in the end it leads to death" (Prov 14:12). *R. E. Speer* remarked [S1], "Men are not in this sad situation because they have not heard the Gospel, but because they are human. They are not sinners because they haven't heard the Gospel. The Gospel would save them, if they would hear it and accept it."

*Oswald Smith*, missionary and author of the bestseller "The Passion for Souls" , wrote [S6, 109]: "If heathens are not lost as long as they have not heard the Gospel, then it would be better to leave them with their lack of knowledge. If only those are damned who with full realisation and will reject Christ, then we should never bring them the Gospel. It would be far better to leave them in the dark, than to bring them under judgment. But the whole Bible teaches us that men without Christ are lost and that their only hope and salvation lies in the Gospel." It is in any case right to preach the Gospel to those who have not heard, since Jesus said, "Therefore go and make disciples off all nations ... teaching them to obey everything I have commanded you" (Matt 28:19-20).

## 10.6  People Who Lived Before Jesus Came: Born Too Soon?

Because the New Testament states so clearly and unambig-uously that there is no salvation without Jesus Christ, many pose the question: what about those people who lived during the Old Testament times? Did they live too early, or did Jesus come to this world as saviour too late? Again the same reasoning applies here as in the previous paragraph: no one is lost because he lived too soon; if men are lost, then this is because of sin and because they did not obey their conscience or the message from God.

The contemporaries of *Noah* died in the Flood because of their evil. They did not listen to God's call: "My Spirit will not contend with man for ever" (Gen 6:3). God also said to Sodom and Gomorrha, that "Their sin is very grievous" (Gen 18:20), and this was the reason for their downfall. God saves people if they repent, as the heathen from Nineveh did (Jonah 3:5-10). What was the basis for salvation during the Old Testament times, when Jesus had not yet purchased salvation at Golgotha? To understand the history of God's salvation of man, we must consider the following interpretative principles shown to us by the Bible:

We cannot understand the New Testament correctly without the Old Testament (see Jesus' allusions to the OT: Matt 21:42; Matt 22:29; John 5:39), and without the New Testament (God's allusion to the new covenant in Jer 31:31) we cannot properly appreciate the occurrences of the Old Testament.

For example, directly after the first sin, reference was made to a future saviour (Gen 3:15). The chain of promises about Jesus' coming (for example, Gen 49:10; Ps 22; Isaiah 53:1-12; Zech 9:9) was not interrupted until the cry, "It is fulfilled" on the cross of Golgotha completed God's plan of salvation. The Bible gives us a look at heaven, where the Old Testament believers are found: "... when you see Abraham, Isaac and Jacob and all the prophets, in the kingdom of God" (Luke 13:28). Their salvation is also based on Jesus' sacrificial death, "It is impossible for the blood of bulls and goats to take away sins (Hebr 10:4). Since without the shedding of blood there can be no forgiveness of sins (Hebr 9:22), the sacrifices of animals during the old covenant gave hints about Jesus, the lamb of God, the perfect sacrifice without blemish. In Hebrews 9:15 it is written that the Old Testament covenant is done away with: "For this reason Christ is the mediator of a new covenant, that those who are called may receive the promised eternal inheritance – now that he has died as a ransom to set them free from the sins committed under the first covenant." *Paul* also confirmed the timeless effect of Jesus' sacrificial death: "God presented him as a sacrifice of atonement, through faith in his blood. He did this to demonstrate his justice, because in his forbearance he had left the sins committed beforehand unpunished – he did it to demonstrate his justice at the present time, so as to be just and the one who justifies the man who has faith in Jesus" (Rom 3:25-26). The people before Christ's time attained salvation in the same manner, through Jesus, if they repented and were obedient to God, as one does today. Hebrews 4:2 implies that the message of salvation was given to people before Christ's coming: "For we also have had the gospel preached to us, just as they did; but the message they heard was of no value to them, because those who heard did not combine it with faith." Three people from the Bible, who belonged to different dispensational periods, will be used to illustrate how they were saved by obedience to God:

**1. Job:** Moses's Law (the Ten Commandments) had not yet been revealed in his time. *Job* acted according to his conscience: "Job ... was blameless and upright; he feared God and shunned evil" (Job 1:1). His trust in God also protected him in times of trouble: "The LORD gave and the LORD has taken away; may the name of the LORD be praised" (Job 1:20)

**2. David:** In his time people were saved by following the Law, or by seeking forgiveness. A conversion to Jesus did not yet exist; however, *David* was "A man after my own heart" (Acts 13:22), since he was humble and repented and changed from his bad deeds.

**3. Lydia:** The way to salvation at the time she lived was acceptance of the Gospel of Jesus Christ. Since God's dispensation towards man was fulfilled in Jesus, there is now only a single way to the father (John 14:6). *Lydia* was a God-fearing woman, who sought after God and worshipped Him, but the new message had not yet reached her area. When she heard Paul's Gospel, she accepted it immediately and was saved (Acts 16:14-15).

These three Biblical characters had a firm belief in God. They did what God told them to do in their time and were saved by it. The true basis of salvation for all of them, however, is Jesus Christ as discussed above.


## 10.7 Many Babies and Children: Died Too Soon?

The Bible speaks of a time of peace during the Millennium, in which all people will reach a blessed old age: "Never again will there be in it an infant that lives but a few days, or an old man who does not live out his years; he who dies at a hundred will be though a mere youth ... They will not toil in vain or bear children doomed to misfortune; for they will be a people, blessed by the Lord, they and their descendants with them" (Isaiah 65:20+23).

In our world today, babies and children sometimes die before they reach an age where they are capable of making decisions and choosing between right and wrong. This occurs due to sickness, famine, war, accidents, abortions, that is, through all the causes of suffering which are found in the world at this time.

Where are the souls of these children after their early demise? There was a doctrine from the Middle Ages which taught that non-baptised children are damned. Does this teaching have any Biblical basis whatsoever? First of all, it is necessary to emphasise that faith in Jesus has saving power, not baptism. Jesus himself made the final statement about children: "Let the little children come to me, and do not hinder them, for the kingdom of God" (Luke 18:16). Babies and small children were brought to Jesus. The disciples found them to be an unnecessary burden

**Figure 17:** *Matthew 18:14: "Even so it is not the will of your Father, who is in heaven, that one of these little ones should perish."*

for the master and a disturbance of their missionary task. But Jesus viewed children in a special way, as heirs to the kingdom of heaven. We conclude, therefore, that children who died "much too soon" are with the Lord.

# 11 What Should We Do?
## Convert and Do Missionary Work!

The Bible clearly states that aside from Jesus there is no other name under heaven through which man can be saved (Acts 4:12). Without Jesus there is no hope. All man's religions are, in the light of the Bible, merely inventions of category (3) according to Chapter 4 (see *Figure 12*), that is, unfortunate false paths invented by people. If people could acquire God's favour through their own righteousness, then the Son of God would not have had to die. The path of religion cannot lead us out of perdition; therefore, God has offered the solution coming from himself and not from man, and that is the only way which can save us from eternal damnation: it is the Gospel of Jesus Christ! If we reject what the Bible tells us about hell, then we can neither come to a correct understanding of the glorious Gospel nor value it enough. The well-meant doctrines that all will be saved or that the Gospel will be preached to those already dead, and others, can be compared to checks filled out for large amounts, which pretend to have a great worth, but which are not covered in God's bank.

**Human imagination or God's ways:** In many situations we are deceived and don't recognise the truth. We mistake our own notions for God's will. If one deceives himself in the matter of salvation, the consequences are most serious. The Bible is full of examples which are intended to warn us about deception, false hopes and false appearances. Based on the people mentioned in the story of the healing of the Syrian captain *Naeman* (2 Kings 5:1-27), who was healed in Israel, the evangelist *Paul Meyer* described the possibilities of false appearances in an impressive way which is useful for our learning. We would like to consider seven people briefly:

- *Naeman*, a successful Syrian captain, was highly regarded by the king and his people due to his glorious deeds. The numerous medals on his uniform were a symbol of power and honour, recognition and popularity. He apparently lacked nothing, but *appearances deceive*: he was leprous!

- The *Jewish woman*, who *Naeman* brought to his wife as a "special souvenir" and useful helper from Israel, was dragged out of her homeland while in her youth. Without contact to her family and homeland and without the usual worship in the temple, she had to live abroad and perform all sorts of lowly tasks. In this situation, one would have expected to find her grim, angry and full of hate towards her master, but *appearances deceive*: she spoke about the living God and reported full of joy about his great prophet, through whom it was possible to obtain help.

- The *king of the Syrians* heard about the possibility of becoming healed by God's prophet, and one would have thought, he would have sent Naeman to him, but *appearances deceive*: he embarked on his own diplomacy and wrote to the *king of Israel* that he would like to have his captain healed. He looked for healing in the wrong place.

- *Naeman* came to the *king of Israel* with a large retinue and rich treasures. The unusual visit should have pleased the king, but *appearances deceive*: the king interpreted all this as a malicious attack against himself.

- *Naeman* hoped that *Elisha*, the prophet of God, would lay his hands on him and pray for him, but *hopes are deceptive*: *Elisha* didn't even show up. He sent only a servant to the door, to impart something totally incomprehensible to *Naeman*: he should wash himself seven times in the dirty Jordan to be cured.

- *Naeman's servants* experienced their master's full wrath, since he had expected a prayer for healing from the prophet, but instead was told to do something unworthy of himself. The servants were used to always agreeing immediately with their warlike captain. One might expect that the servants would have accepted his opinion as usual, but *appearances deceive*: they took the side of the prophet and attempted to convince *Naeman* to undergo the unusual treatment. The captain was certainly prepared to offer a rich payment or to perform a glorious deed as a prerequisite to being healed, but he distrusted the free cure, because of the humbling step of obedience required.

- *Gehasi* spent a long time as a Bible student of the greatest prophet in Israel. He was well instructed in the Holy Scriptures and knew what was pleasing to God. He saw the healed *Naeman* return to the house of the prophet, and *Naeman* wished to reward him with money and goods. In spite of the Bible school's great poverty, *Elisha* let him go, since *Elisha* wished to teach him an important lesson: God's healing does not cost anything and is based on grace: it is to be accepted in obedience. *Gehasi* should have understood that, but *appearances deceive*: on his own authority, he hurried after the caravan to take advantage of *Naeman's* wealth. Greed and stinginess led him to disaster: God judged him with leprosy.

These examples make clear that people sometimes act in totally unexpected ways. We often believe we are doing what is right, when we are actually deceived. The most tragic human situation is when one believes one is on the right path to God and labours under this misconception (Prov 16:25). He considers himself a believer, but this is only appearance.

He is

- one, who as a so-called "honourable man", at least in his own opinion, "does righteous and fears no man". He boasts to have never murdered anyone, to have never performed adultery, and so a "God of love" will never cast him out. But *appearances deceive*, the Sermon on the Mount unmasks those with such attitudes as being lost in their own self-righteousness;

126

- one, who lives in a self-created security. He has even done many deeds in the name of Jesus, but *appearances deceive*: the door to the Kingdom of Heaven remains closed to him, since he has concentrated only on himself instead of seeking God's will. Jesus will have to say to him, "I never knew you. Away from me, you evildoers" (Matt 7:23);

- one, who claims to also believe in God. Should someone dispute it with him, he will defend himself vigorously. But *appearances deceive*: he has never been converted and is therefore lost;

- one, who has heard the Gospel and considers Christianity a good thing. He offers immediately to go into the mission field, but *appearances deceive*: without conversion, no one can serve the Lord as a missionary. The second step cannot be carried out before the first.

Too often we misjudge; therefore, we should examine ourselves to see which of the following two groups we belong in and then take appropriate action:

**One Not Yet Saved**: The message from Lamentations 3:40 is relevant here: "Let us examine our ways and test them, and let us return to the Lord." Salvation is the message the bible is aiming to teach. Every man is called upon to accept the salvation offered by Jesus. "Through him everyone who believes is justified from everything" (Acts 13:39). To the jailer's question, "What must I do to be saved?" (Acts 16:30) the answer was given which is also relevant to us: "Believe in the Lord Jesus!" (Acts 16:31). Turning to Jesus Christ in repentance and conversion, and faith from the heart on the son of God saves believers from being lost and leads them to eternal life. Whoever accepts Jesus experiences great changes in his life and becomes a doer instead of an observer. We read about the new relationship of the jailer: "And the whole family was filled with joy, because they had come to believe in God" (Acts 16:34). If we don't yet believe, Jesus' word applies to us, "Go and do likewise" (Luke 10:37).

**The saved**: If we have been converted, then God has entrusted us with the greatest and most beautiful task there is. Since "We are therefore Christ's ambassadors" (2 Cor 5:20). This service is characterised in three ways:

a) **Gratefulness for our salvation at Golgotha**: Since we ourselves have been saved, out of gratefulness, we must win other people to the faith. People who are grateful to God labour differently from people who think they have no reason to be grateful. The possibilities are different for each person, but God can use everyone.

b) **Service of love**: Every service for the kingdom of God can only occur properly through love towards Jesus (John 21:16). All efforts for the Lord must therefore have this love as their driving force.

c) **Service as an ambassador commissioned by God**: The Lord has called upon us to serve him: "For we are God's fellow-workers" (1 Cor 3:9). What does it mean to labour? Employer and employee share an interdependent relationship. Like, he cannot do without me, and I cannot do without him. One thing is clear: we cannot do anything without God. Does the opposite apply in relationships with God: can he do nothing without us? It is unimaginable for us that the almighty God should be dependent on us humans. Is he really dependent on our work? God did not need man to create the huge universe out of nothing through his almighty word (Hebr 11:3), and he created life, but he commissioned man to fill the earth, to preserve it and to conquer it. God **alone** did the redemptive work. Jesus hung abandoned by God on the cross. He **alone** carried the guilt of the world and fulfilled the redemption, but he uses us as fellow-workers to tell the message of salvation. He commissioned us to spread this message (Matt 28:19-20; Mark 16:15-16; Acts 1:8).

What we do not do remains undone since:

"How, then, can they call on the one
they have not believed in?
And how can they believe in one
of whom they have not heard?
And how can they hear without someone preaching to
them?" (Rom 10:14).
"Consequently, faith comes from hearing the message,
and the message is heard through the word of Christ"
(Rom 10:17).

In a brochure from the *Wycliff Bible Translators* the following
discussion between an Indian and a missionary, which should
cause us to contemplate, was printed:

"When you were only a child, did you already know about
Jesus?" an Indian asked me.
"Yes" , I answered him.
"Then your father also knew about him?"
"Yes."
"And your grandfather?"
" ... "
The Indian remained silent a long time.
Finally, he said, "My father and grandfather would have
liked very much to have known about him. Why did you
wait so long to come?"

We are his fellow-workers, his ambassadors, his commissioned
workers. He gives us the strength needed to do the work, he
motivates us with his love and gives us the desire to rescue the
lost. God uses neither angels nor other beings to announce the
Gospel. He uses **us,** according to his plan. *It is the most
important task a person can ever be assigned to do.*

As I stood before the Great Wall in China during a trip to the
Far East, I could do nothing but marvel. This construction is
about 5000 km long and is the only project undertaken in this
world which can be seen from the moon with bare eyes. A
Chinese emperor commissioned this work to be carried out.

After about a century of building, this task, which involved only the north border of China, was finished. Yet this wall now has no more value, except as a tourist attraction.

God's commission is entirely different:

- **It is the task of most extensive size**: It reaches from the person right next to us to the end of the world. There are people everywhere who need the Gospel. Wherever we go, whether within the country or abroad, we go as Christ's ambassadors. We have the possibility to be living witnesses, "Epistles of Christ" (2 Cor 3:3), through personal discussions or through spiritual literature. (Foreign language literature can be requested for various lands from missionary boards.)

- **It is the task covering the most extensive timespan**: No other task has ever been assigned with a longer timespan as the task of spreading the message of the Gospel. As long as the world exists, God will send out people with his message. In the breaking of the bread during the Lord's Supper, we read, "Proclaim the Lord's death until he comes" (1 Cor 11:26). Only with the Lord's Second Coming does the missionary command terminate.

- **It is a task with eternal effects**: Human tasks are characterised by their temporariness. What once was an important matter becomes unimportant after some generations, or often even after a few years, and is forgotten. The Kingdom of God is quite different. Even the glass of cold water which we give a disciple in the name of Jesus has eternal value (Matt 10:42). How much greater will the everlasting joy be if we have helped people to find the way to the father's house.

All sorts of labour are important. The Bible clarifies this with the imagery of agriculture and construction: plowing, sowing, planting, watering, harvesting. A broad range of activities is presented, in which all sorts of talents can be used. This service should not be done carelessly (Jer 48:10); God expects us to apply all our personality and means at our disposal to this task. *David Livingstone* (1813-1873), a missionary and researcher on Africa, witnessed about himself: "What I have and own is only valuable to me in so far as it can serve to spread the kingdom of God." All capabilities, activities and possibilities are to be used. God seeks our loyalty and needs our creativity. *Oswald Smith* described our actions with three words [S6]: donation, prayer, participation. We will be either givers, who help with the financial requirements of missionary service abroad and at home, or we will be active ourselves in spreading the Gospel. In any case, it is good if spreading the message of the kingdom of God is accompanied by personal prayer. The three words mentioned above are not mutually exclusive duties, but can complement each other.

**Figure 18:** *Tribal Mission with the Dumagats in the Philippine jungle on the main island of Luzon (Missionary Helmut Keller, Deutsche Missions- Gemeinschaft).*

*Karl Lagershausen* (*Overseas Mission*) stated about prayer for missionary work [O1, 59]: "A prayer which reaches around the world is better than a self-centred one. As Christians we should also be realistic. In any case, I do not wish to ever be outside of the world-wide fellowship of those praying." It must be emphasised that personal action is not superfluous: "Money and prayer are no substitute for direct participation. One also prays away from home. Only the sacrifice of one's life makes the money offering acceptable."

We are guilty, if we do not labour in God's commission: "This is a day of good news and we are keeping it to ourselves. If we wait until daylight, punishment will overtake us" (2 Kings 7:9).

If we accept Jesus' commission in this world and fulfil it loyally with all the talents available to us, then we may rejoice on the day of his glorious return, when he will say, "Well done, good and faithful servant! You have been faithful with a few things; I will put you in charge of many things. Come and share your master's happiness!" (Matt 25:21).

# 12 Heaven: Our Goal!

In the preceding chapters, we have dealt with the question of **how** one gets to heaven and **who** goes to heaven. Using the Bible, we have recognised that the all-will-be-saved doctrine in the words of the German carnival song "We shall all go to heaven!" is a lie. We shall now discuss what those who receive the inheritance of heaven can expect.

The Bible does not leave us in the dark about the place of our eternal destiny. It is the *only* source of information about heaven. We must first reject all human notions about heaven, before considering God's revelation.

Heaven is not:

- the "Happy Hunting Ground" of the Indians
- the "Land of the Silver Sky" of the Babylonians
- the "Underworld" or the "Island of the Blessed" of the Greeks
- the "Life of Luxury" of the Mohammedan
- the "Shadowy Kingdom of the Dead" of the Egyptians
- the "Nirvana" of the Buddhists.

In spite of the manifold differences – ranging from the beliefs of primitive bush people to those of "cultured" people – all religions share something in common: they all sense eternity. We would like to clarify why that is so using a little story told so graphically by *Richard Wurmbrand* [W2]:

"One day in the fall, a crow had a conversation with a young swallow less than a year old. The crow said to the swallow, 'I see you are preparing for a long trip. Where are you going to fly to?' The swallow answered, 'It will become cold here. I could freeze to death. I am going to fly to a warmer land.' The crow replied mockingly, 'But consider your birth. You were only born here a few months ago. How can you know that there is a warmer land which will offer you protection when it gets colder?' The swallow replied, 'The one who placed the wish for a warmer climate in my heart cannot have deceived me. I believe him and will fly away.' And the swallow found what it was looking for."

Man is more than a swallow! Psalm 8:5 describes man's situation in view of God's creation: "You made him a little lower than the heavenly beings and crowned him with glory and honour." Even after the fall in sin, man's perception of eternity has remained. It is programmed into each person, as the Old Testament says: "He has made everything beautiful in its time. He has also set eternity in the hearts of men" (Eccl 3:11). The witness from various people confirms this claim in the Bible [R1]. But eternity remains only a perception. People have described this perception colourfully with their imagination, according to the various environments in which they lived. Thus, the hunting-oriented Indians imagined eternity as a hunting ground with an unmeasurable wealth of game. *Mohammed's* concept of heaven agrees entirely with the taste of an Arab, who lives in a desert. Even the Communist revolutionary *Ho Chi Minh* (1890-1969) believed in life after death. When after his death his testament was read before prominent communists, the following sentence was found: "I am going there, to meet comrades *Marx*, *Lenin* and *Engels*." The heathen poet *Hermann Löns* (1866-1914) witnessed in his own way his perception of eternity:

"I know of a land, in which I have never been;
Water flows there, which is silvery clear,
Flowers bloom there, whose aroma is so pure,
And their colours are so tender and fine ...
A bird also sings in that faraway land,
It sings a song, which to me is unknown;
I never heard it before and yet know how it sounds,
And also know what the bird sings to me;
He sings about life, and he sings about death,

The highest bliss and the deepest unhappiness,
All desires and every heartache,
The desires of time, the pain of eternity ...
If I reach that faraway, foreign land,
Then blooms my life in my hand;
If not, then the bird only sang of death,
Sang of a life, bitter and full of unhappiness."

The entire wealth of those living in heaven lies, however, far beyond our ability to imagine. Therefore, *Paul* wrote about what God knows: "No eye has seen, no ear has heard, no mind has conceived what God has for those who love him" (1 Cor 2:9). How great the surprise will be for those who inherit heaven, when the transformation from faith to sight occurs. When the *queen of Sheba* saw amazed the wealth and glory of **Solomon**, she acknowledged: "Indeed, not even half the greatness of your wisdom was told me" (2 Chron 9:6). How much more does that apply to Jesus' followers, who someday will see and inherit his kingdom. God has nevertheless opened a crack in the door with respect to heaven with his Word, in order to give us a taste of the glory to come. Some details have been summarised here.

## 12.1 Heaven: The Father's House

When the Lord Jesus explained to the disciples that he was leaving to prepare places to dwell in, he said, "In my father's house are many rooms" (John 14:2). Heaven is God's abode as demonstrated by several portions in the Bible:

Genesis 24:7:    "The Lord, the God of heaven."
Nehemiah 1:5:    "Then I said: O Lord, God of heaven."
Psalms 115:3:    "Our God is in heaven."
Psalms 115:16:   "The highest heavens belong to the Lord."
Matthew 6:9:     "Our Father in heaven."

Heaven is also Jesus' place of abode: from there, he came to us in the world (John 3:13; John 6:38) and after his Ascension, he returned there (Luke 24:51; Acts 1:11). During his last hours together with his disciples, he said that he was going to the Father. He will return from there to meet those who belong to him.

Man's situation is miserable, if he does not have a home, if his sense of security has been removed. Even the nihilist philosopher *Friedrich Nietzsche* (1844-1900), who coined the phrase "God is dead", complained about homelessness:

> "The world – a gate
> to a thousand deserts, mute and cold!
> he who loses,
> what you lost, can stop nowhere.
> Now you stand, pale,
> cursed to winter wandering,
> like smoke,
> which always seeks colder heavens ...
> **Woe to he who has no home!**"

Even if someone owned all the treasures and riches of the world, possessed all honours and titles, and were to be furnished with everything, he would still have nothing in the end. Nothing can satisfy the heart, it remains in spite of all earthly treasures empty, deceived and homeless, if Jesus is not the central point. God has built a need for a home within man. The final home is with God himself. In this passing world, we do not have a lasting home town (Hebr 13:14). We remain "aliens and strangers" (1 Peter 2:11) in this world, since "Our citizenship is in heaven" (Phil 3:20). Heaven is the eternal home. It is the place of eternal life, the abode of the saved. Heaven is there, where Jesus is. Jesus' expressed wish is, "Where I am, my servant also will be" (John 12:26). In the well-known prayer in John 17 the Lord prayed, "Father, I want those you have given me to be with me where I am, and to see my glory!" (John 17:24).

## 12.2  Heaven: the Place of Eternal Love

God's character is love, and, therefore, heaven is also a place of eternal love. *Faith*, *hope*, *love*, these three things are central matters for a Christian, "But the greatest of these is love" (1 Cor 13:13). *Faith* will end when replaced by sight. *Hope* also ends in eternity, since it will then be fulfilled, but "*Love* never fails" (1 Cor 13:8). The greatest love has been demonstrated by the Lord himself, in that he, who was God, became man and died in our place on the cross: "Greater love has no-one than this, that one lay down his life for his friends" (John 15:13). He has also commissioned us with the command to love. It is a wide spectrum, ranging from our brothers to our enemies. No one can be a Believer who does not love Jesus with his whole heart. The Lord requests a sign of recognition: "If anyone loves me, he will obey my teaching" (John 14:23). He did not ask Peter a question about his knowledge or eloquence, but about his love: "Do you love me?" (John 21:17). People often abandon what they like, but almost never what they love. They can deny what they believe in with their mind, but never what lies deep in their hearts. *Charles H. Spurgeon* (1834-1892) emphasised [S8,27], "As long as you live, do everything out of love for Christ. Let your fingers do works of love, let the brain, the eyes, and the hands express love, fight with love, pray in love, speak in love, live with love."

Heaven is a place of complete love. God himself is personified love, and he will fill the whole heaven with it. Someone asked a young boy what he thought heaven was. He recognised the character of heaven correctly: "The place where everyone loves everyone!"

## 12.3  Heaven: No Longer Cursed

Whereas our world is influenced by man's fall into sin, in heaven, "No longer will there be any curse" (Rev 22:3). Everything will be perfect (1 Cor 13:10), and nothing will remain to remind us about the abyss of sin. God himself will make everything new: "He will wipe every tear from their eyes. There will be no more death or mourning or crying or pain, for the old order of things has passed away" (Rev 21:4). All things which burden us will be permanently banished. We will have truly fulfilled lives. We will not miss anything. There will no longer be anything which one could still somehow change or improve. Everything will be perfect. Clocks will no longer put us under pressure and remind us of our limited time. The temporal will be dissolved in the eternal. The question, "Where is God?" will no longer be asked, since God will be among us. There will no longer be doubters, since faith will be replaced by actual sight. We will see God face to face. There will no longer be fear of the future, since the future will become eternaly present. There will no longer be a need for comforting, since all sorrowing people will be happy. We will only smile compassionately, when we think about death, because this will be a problem which we have overcome. There will be no crying any more, since no one will suffer any lack. There will be no more sin, the cause of all pain and suffering. The new creation will have no evidence of sin. The gates of the city will no longer need to be closed, since there will no longer be thieves. There will be no police, no seaches, no prisons, no bolts or locks. There will be no undertakers and graves, since each inhabitant will have eternal life. There will be no doctors or clinics, since bacteria, fever, epidemics and sicknesses will be unknown. There will be no Red Cross, no emergency stations or surgeons, no accidents or natural catastrophes, and wars will be a thing of the past. There will be no destroyed communities, since there will be no alcoholics, no drug or pill addicts. There will be no beggars, no blind, deaf, dumb, or lame people. There will be no language barriers, or difference in race or education, no hostility, no self-centredness and no greed, since, "We shall be like him, for we shall see him as he is" (1 John 3:2).

What a land! Just thinking of it fills us with longing and home-sickness.

## 12.4 Heaven: the Eternal Feast of Joy

It is no coincidence that Jesus performed his first miracle during a wedding (John 2:1-11). A wedding is always a special occasion of joy. In my old East Prussian homeland weddings were not celebrated only a single day, but as a rule, the celebration lasted three days. Heaven is also a wedding feast, but not of a limited duration. Jesus, the lamb of God, who once carried the sins of the world, patient as a lamb, is the groom, and his church – his saved flock coming from all peoples, tribes and nations of the earth – is the bride. Joy will abound: "Let us rejoice and be glad and give him glory! For the wedding of the Lamb has come, and his bride has made herself ready" (Rev 19:7). In the parable of the prodigal son we read, "So they began to celebrate" (Luke 15:24). In heaven this happiness does not stop, and we cannot imagine the measure of joy. *C. H. Spurgeon* said [S8, 150], "Our joy on earth is hardly more than low tide, but in heaven the joy will rush in like high tide." Here joy is a fruit of the spirit (Gal 5:22), and *Paul* admonished us in Christ, to always rejoice (Phil 4:4). There is nothing comparable to heavenly joy here; therefore, the prophet refers to perfect joy.

By looking forward to heaven, earthly pain is melted: "I consider that our present sufferings are not worth comparing with the glory that will be revealed in us" (Rom 8:18). Even when we are plagued by temptation and persecution, the anticipation of eternal happiness can help us to endure: "Do not be surprised at the painful trial you are suffering, as though something strange were happening to you. But rejoice that you participate in the suffering of Christ, so that you may be overjoyed when his glory is revealed." (1 Peter 4:12-13). Joy is the climate of heaven; by the Lord we will have "Fullness of joy" (Ps 16:11). What a wonderful moment, when the Lord upon his return says to his loyal servants, "Come and share your master's happiness!" (Matt 25:21). At the Lord's wedding table, the unimaginable will occur: he will serve us as his guests: "He will dress himself to serve, will have them recline at the table and will come and wait on them" (Luke 12:37). The creator of the universe and all life, the Son of God in his majesty and glory, who did everything for us to redeem us, will serve us. I hardly dare write the thought down, but the Lord Himself has said it.

**Figure 19:** "... *a great multitude that no-one could count, from every nation, tribe, people and language" (Rev 7:9).*

In the parable of the great banquet (Luke 14:16-24), the Lord shows us how he seeks guests for the eternal wedding. Everyone is invited to the greatest and most beautiful wedding: to be a guest of Jesus. Have you ever experienced how it is, wanting to do something good for someone and receiving the cold shoulder? How much worse it would be to turn down the invitation to the feast of all feasts! "Then the owner of the house became angry ..." (Luke 14:21). Those who turn it down, with any of a thousand mundane excuses, will never see heaven. Will heaven thus remain empty? No, the wedding feast will have a full table. The Lord Jesus described his guests as coming from all lands: "People will come from east and west and north and south, and will take their places at the feast in the kingdom of God" (Luke 13:29). On earth they belonged to various different peoples and races, but in heaven they comprise the single family of God, who *John* was allowed to see: "After this I looked and there before me was a great multitude that no-one could count, from every nation, tribe, people and language, standing before the throne and in front of the Lamb. They were wearing white robes" (Rev 7:9).

**His** hour came at the wedding in Canaan. The Lord calls us today: **your** hour has come to accept the invitation to the wedding of the lamb, to the feast of eternal joy.

## 12.5  Heaven: Sun without a Sunset

The last book in the Old Testament refers to the eternal sun:

> "But for you that who revere my name, the sun of righteousness will rise" (Mal 4:2).

The Lord Jesus is himself the sun. His glorious return is a sunrise for the believers. Shortly before this sunrise of eternity, "The sun will be darkened, and the moon will not give its light" (Matt 24:29). Their temporary task will have been fulfilled: "... For the first heaven and the first earth had passed away" (Rev 21:1). The new has dawned.

The current creation receives its light from a created sun. Light is an indispensable prerequisite for life. God's character is light (1 John 1:5), therefore, light is also an essential characteristic of the new creation. There will no longer be a created sun; the

Lord himself will be the light. *Isaiah* was able to prophesy this: "The sun will no more be your light by day, nor will the brightness of the moon shine on you, for the Lord will be your everlasting light, and your God will be your glory. Your sun will never set again, and your moon will wane no more; the Lord will be your everlasting light, and your days of sorrow will end" (Isaiah 60:19-20).

In the last two chapters of the Bible, it is revealed that Jesus *was* not only the light of the world (John 8:12), but *is* also the light of eternity: "The city does not need the sun or the moon to shine on it, for the glory of God gives it light, and the Lamb is its lamp" (Rev 21:23). The Lamb of God, who once carried the sins of the world, appears now in all eternity as the sun of righteousness. We are now programmed into a day-night rhythm. In heaven there "will be no more night" (Rev 22:5).

The German-Roman emperor *Karl V* was between 1516-1556 simultaneously *Karl I,* the king of Spain. He conquered Mexico and Peru and laid thereby the foundation for the Spanish colonial kingdom. His reign went from middle America to Spain. He said proudly:

"In my land the sun never sets!"

Actually the statement was not correct, but in any case, his kingdom has long since perished. One can, however, really say this about God's kingdom, heaven: It is the only "Land" where *"The sun never sets"*.

# 13 Concluding Remarks

In this book, we have dealt with a topic which is relevant today, often leading to serious discussions. Due to international travel and information flow from the mass media, we are constantly confronted with various religions. The penetrating question then arises: don't all the various religious paths lead to salvation and automatically bring people to an eternity with God? Won't God recognise that in their own ways, they have tried? Doesn't truth have many faces?

*Lessing* wrote the *Parable of the Ring* (Nathan the Wise) which criticised the uniqueness of the Gospel. Even prominent church representatives have accepted this false doctrine. Recently an article with the title "Is God to Be Found in All Religions?" appeared in the "Idea-Spektrum" (H. 12/91 from March 20, 91, p.7), the well-known information magazine of the Evangelical Alliance. There one reads, "The director of the Protestant Academy in Loccum, *Hans May*, expressed his wish regarding the term 'Claim to Absolutism' (of Christianity), since he views it as belonging to an imperialistic and colonial category: 'Who are we to claim to have absolute truth?' Instead, he thought, one should speak of a 'competition for truth among religions' ... According to the theologist Professor *Theo Sundermeier* from the University of Heidelberg, all religions belong to 'God's dealing with the world'." A cartoon added by "Idea-spektrum" (four children sit with questioning looks around their father) reacted appropriately to this anti-Biblical statement, in which the children asked, "Dad, why are we only *your* children? Come on, give up your absolute claim on us!"

Furthermore, as already discussed in Chapter 10, many "Christian" teachers teach special ways to be saved. The tragedy of salvation alternatives invented by humans – independent of whether they are expressed in religious terms or in the current Christian jargon – is in their terrible deception: one thinks one is heading for life, but one, is actually lost, because of the deceitful false doctrine (e. g. Jude 4+11).

We have attempted to answer the pertinent questions in light of the revelations in the Word of God. This book is intended to inform both those searching for answers and those who already believe. Sometimes we quoted people who are true witnesses of the Word. It is more important, however, that God Himself speaks to us richly through His Word. What God has conveyed to us, we strive to emphasise; where He says nothing, we have also refrained from expressing ourselves. From the witness of the Scriptures, we can recognise that error has many faces, but the truth has only one. There are many paths to damnation, but only one to salvation. It is clear, through Jesus' discussion with *Pilate* (John 18:33-38) that truth is neither many-sided nor unreachable. It is in the person of the Son of God, to be accepted or rejected.

The difference between religion and the Gospel has also been nicely expressed by the Canadian evangelist *Leo Janz*:

"There are thousands of religions, but only one Gospel.
Religions have all been thought up by man; the Gospel, however, is a revelation of God's thoughts.
Religions were made by man; the Gospel, however, is a gift from God.
Religions are human opinions; the Gospel is God's communication to us.
Religion, generally speaking, has a history behind it of sinful people, who wish to do something for the holy God; the Gospel, however, tells us what the holy God has done for sinful people.
Religion is a search for God; the Gospel, however, is the good news that Jesus is searching for people: the Son of Man has come, to seek and save what is lost.
The best religion tends to emphasise the importance of exterior things; the Gospel, however, begins with an inner change."

We have offered a detailed, stepwise explanation of how man's salvation through the Gospel comes about. One has no right to salvation; what the Gospel provides us with is grace. It is not our place to judge God's judgment according to our standards; some may think "How unsearchable his judgments, and his paths beyond tracing out!" (Rom 11:33). Fortunately, his Word is available as an immutable document. You should verify our explanations using the Holy Scriptures and act accordingly.

# APPENDIX

## Is There Another Chance to Be Saved after Death?

Continuing the discussion in Chapter 10.1, we wish to examine two passages which are occasionally considered to be evidence that the Gospel can be preached to the dead.

### 1 The passage Ephesians 4:8-10

"This is why it says: (Ps 68:19) When he ascended on high, he led captives in his train and gave gifts to men. (What does 'he ascended' mean except that he also descended to the lower, earthy regions? He who descended is the very one who ascended higher than all the heavens, in order to fill the whole universe) (Eph 4:8-10)."

These statements were already considered important by the early Christians, and the Apostolical Statement of Faith goes:

"... crucified, dead and buried,
descended to the kingdom of the dead,
risen on the third day from the dead,
ascended into heaven ..."

Still, we cannot conclude from the text above that Jesus preached to the dead. The text makes no such statement. Rather, the immeasurable extent of Jesus' victory, is emphasised: he has gone through everything, from the deepest depth up to heaven, before assuming his lordship over all. Colossians 2:15 describes this victory as a triumph over **all** powers: "And having disarmed the powers and authorities, he made a public spectacle of them, triumphing over them by the cross." After the crucifixion, the Lord's body lay three days and three nights in the heart of the earth (Matt 12:40). From this depth, he rose. He alone had the power over both death and the kingdom of the dead (Rev 1:18). In his *victory* every imaginable power has been swallowed up (1 Cor 15:55). He has truly been given "all authority in heaven and on earth" (Matt 28:18). Everyone must bow and submit before this *king of kings*. Even if today many powers are still in effect, the day will come when "at the name of Jesus every knee should bow, in heaven and on earth and under the earth" (Phil 2:10).

## 2  The passage 1 Peter 3:18-20

This passage is one of the most difficult in the New Testament.

> "For Christ died for sins once for all, the righteous for the unrighteous, to bring you to God. He was put to death in the body but made alive by the Spirit, through whom also he went and preached to the spirits in prison who disobeyed long ago when God waited patiently in the days of Noah while the ark was being built. In it only a few people, eight in all, were saved through water" (1 Peter 3:18-20).

**1. Introduction:** Various revisions of Bible translations into English have produced no significant changes in this Bible passage; nevertheless, interpretations of this passage have led to many speculative statements which go far beyond what is written. In his review, *Jürgen Kuberski* [K5] compared five different interpretations. Here, we would like to restrict ourselves to what we think the Biblical text tells us. It is difficult, because there are no parallel texts in the Bible. For *Luther* a lot remained in the dark: "That is the most peculiar and dark text, which appears in the New Testament, so that I don't know with certainty what *Saint Peter* meant."

We can determine that in the original Greek text the words for "went" (*poreutheis*) "preached" (*ekeeryxen*) and "not obey" (*apeitheesain*) are expressed in the aorist grammatical form, that is, it deals with a matter which occurred in the past and is terminated. "Spirits in prison" are the spirits of the dead in the kingdom of the dead. According to the witness of the Scriptures, they are not inactive beings nor diffused nothings, but find themselves in a real existence, are capable of remembering (Luke 16:28) and of perception (Luke 16:23-24). We would like to present the interpretation here which appears consistent with the complete witness of the Scriptures, that is: even at the time of Noah, people were preached to in "the spirit of Christ" (1 Peter 1:11).

**2. Preaching in the Spirit of Christ:** When the Lord Jesus lived on earth, God spoke directly to man, without needing a person as his tool. Before and after His time on earth, men called by God acted in "the spirit of Christ" . The spirit of Christ was active both through teachings of the Old Testament prophets (1 Peter 1:10-11) and through preaching the Gospel after His return to heaven. As an example, Christ did not personally go to people in Ephesus; however, one reads "He came and preached peace to you" (Eph 2:17). Christ did this through *Paul*, who had the spirit of Christ. Jesus said to the disciples, "He who listens to you listens to me" (Luke 10:16).

In a similar manner, it was preached to the disobedient contemporaries of *Noah*. For 120 years they heard the call to repentance of the "*preacher of righteousness*" (2 Peter 2:5). The "*spirit of Christ*" lived and acted through *Noah* (1 Peter 1:11). It was thus Christ who through *Noah* admonished to repentance. In spite of God's patience, man remained disobedient. Now *Noah's* contemporaries find themselves in the kingdom of the dead and await judgment like all those without God (2 Peter 2:3-6). In the rabbinical tradition, the Flood generation was also seen as completely and hopelessly lost. Preaching is by nature also an offer of salvation. Since the lost have already been judged, preaching to the Flood generation would not agree with other Biblical doctrines. This conclusion is further supported by the following text from 1 Peter 4:5-6: "But they will have to give account to him who is ready to judge the living and the dead. For this is the reason the gospel was preached even to those who are now dead, so that they might be judged according to men in regard to the body, but live according to God in regard to the spirit." Here also the aorist grammatical form is used, that is, those now dead had the good news preached unto them at a specific time during their lives. The text mentioned makes no statement that the Gospel will be preached to the dead either now or later. Another point seems important to understanding the text mentioned above: why exactly are *Noah's* contemporaries mentioned here?

**3. The Flood, a key example of God's warning**: The Flood is dealt with several times in the New Testament and serves as a poignant example of how God warns people. In 2 Peter 2:4-7 the damned and the saved are compared. Three groups of lost souls are emphasised:

- the fallen angels
- the generation lost in the Great Flood
- the inhabitants of Sodom and Gomorrha.

Only eight souls were saved from the Flood and only *Lot* and his two daughters survived the fiery judgment of the two cities. Lot's wife was also rescued; however, she died anyway because of disobedience. These events should convey to us a grave lesson, which is:

- "Made them an example of what is going to happen to the ungodly" (2 Peter 2:6). God's word with respect to salvation and judgment will be unconditionally fulfilled.

- The examples show that God's judgment occurs even when only a small minority is saved. The importance of God's Word should not be ignored.

The Lord Jesus used both judgments "In the days of *Noah*" (Luke 17:26) and "In the days of *Lot*" (Luke 17:28) as warning examples of how it will be at the time of His second coming.

People will be so occupied with daily things such as "eating, drinking, marrying and being given in marriage" , that they will forget God. The same statement will be made about the future judgment: "... and destroyed them all" (Luke 17:27+29). Only God's flock saved through faith will survive. That was true about *Noah's* time and also now.

The Word of God particularly emphasises the saved in the judgments of the past. Verse 21 follows the text that we considered in 1 Peter 3:18-20: "This water symbolises baptism that now saves you also – not the removal of dirt from the body but the pledge of a good conscience towards God. It saves you by the resurrection of Jesus Christ." Those who hear and obey God's call and come to the place of salvation will be saved. At the time of *Noah,* eight souls were "saved from the water". God had ordered the ark to be built to save people from the water. The ark and water act as synonyms here: the ark for salvation, water for death. So baptism in the New Testament refers to that Old Testament event. Whoever delivers himself fully to Christ and is baptised in Christ's death (Rom 6:3) is saved. Thus, the text in 1 Peter 3:18-20 takes on a broader meaning: The New Testament baptism can be viewed as a symbol of the salvation of souls from the Flood.

**4. False doctrines:** The well-known Bible teacher, *H. L. Heij-koop*, wrote about the Bible text under consideration [H1, 333+335]: "There is hardly a portion of God's Word which has so often been ripped out of its context and been misused than these verses ... The main line of logic followed by most of the false doctrines about these verses is that: Christ went to Hades in his human spirit or soul and preached there, between the time of his death and resurrection, while his body still lay in the grave; according to some, to announce the certainty of the coming judgment, according to others to bring the message of the fulfilled work of redemption. But the view most widely shared is that he announced the Gospel to the non-believers, and not only to those who died during the Flood, so that they could still be saved."

If the text in 1 Peter 3:18-20 was supposed to imply to us that there would be a general proclamation in the kingdom of the dead, then it would say that, "So Christ preached the Gospel to the spirits in prison, to those who during their lives had not heard God's Word", or, "Christ preached the Gospel to the spirits in prison, to those who lived in Tyre and Sidon" . Unlike those during the Flood, they had no preacher. Also, in the story about the *rich man* in Luke 16:19-31 no mention is made about an expected proclamation with the possibility of making a decision and being redeemed: "Father Abraham, have pity on me" . Quite the opposite, his situation is explained by referring back to his attitude on earth during his lifetime. We can see the only purpose for mentioning the Flood generation is that which we mentioned above in point 3.

**Let's summarise:** We can now state the following about both the Bible passages Ephesians 4:8-10 and 1 Peter 3:18-20:

- Christ descended "in the heart of the earth" between his crucifixion and resurrection (Matt 12:40; Rom 10:7; Eph 4:8-10). The Bible does not mention any kind of activity done there. In the texts in question, 1 Corinthians 15:55+57, Colossians 2:15 and Revelation 1:18, it is not stated directly, but one could conclude that a general proclamation of Jesus' victory occurred.

- We cannot extract from these sparse texts that an evangelical proclamation to the dead occurred for the purpose of announcing a chance to be saved. *Peter* characterised *Noah's* contemporaries "*as disobedient*". One can only say that about people who had some knowledge of God's will. God waited patiently. They received an unusually long time to repent, but they remained stubborn, and that compounded the people's guilt. They remained disobedient the whole time (120 years) despite the visible reminder before their eyes: the building of the ark. God's judgment came into full effect only after the people allowed their time to run out without repenting.

- We agree with the comment made in the *Scofield* Bible about 1 Peter 3:19:"This means that Christ preached by the Holy Spirit through *Noah* to unsaved people in Old Testament times (1 Peter 1:10-11), their spirits being now in prison. The theory that the Lord Jesus, after His crucifixion, preached to the unsaved dead in hades and gave them a second chance cannot be found in the Scripture".

- If there were another chance to make a decision to accept Jesus after death, surely the Bible would not be silent about such an important matter. The Bible states clearly, however, that we go through this life only once and that then the judgment comes: "Just as man is destined to die once, and after that to face judgment" (Hebr 9:27).

# Literature References

[B1] Bamm, P.: Eines Menschen Einfälle
Droemer Knaur, 6th edition 1978, 126 pages

[B2] Beck, H. W.: Schritte über Grenzen zwischen Technik und
Theologie, Hänssler Publ., Neuhausen-Stuttgart
1979, 255 pages

[B3] Bellinger, G. J.: Knaurs großer Religionsführer
Droemer Knaur, 1990, 431 pages

[B4] Busch, W.: Verkündigung im Angriff
Aussaat Publ., Wuppertal 1968, 196 pages

[B5] Busch, W.: Man muß doch darüber sprechen
Quell Publ., Stuttgart 1950, 21st edition 1987,
91 pages

[D1] Deutsches
Patentamt: Blatt für Patent-, Muster- und Zeichenwesen,
given by the German Patent Office, 92.Jahrgg.,
March 1990

[G1] Gitt, W.: Das biblische Zeugnis der Schöpfung Hänssler
Publ., Neuhausen-Stuttgart, 5th edition 1993,
188 pages

[G1] Gitt, W.: Did God Use Evolution?
Christliche Literatur-Verbreitung, Bielefeld 1993,
160 pages

[G3] Gitt, W.: Questions I have always wanted to ask
Christliche Literatur-Verbreitung, Bielefeld 1992,
157 pages

[G4] Gitt, W.: If Animals Could Talk
Christliche Literatur-Verbreitung, Bielefeld 1994,
124 pages

[H1] Heijkoop, H. L.: Der erste Brief von Petrus
Publ. E. Paulus, Neustadt/Weinstr. 1966

[H2] Herrman, K.: Der Dampfspatenpflug
Kultur & Technik, H. 1, 1981, p. 26-31

[J1] Jessen, J.: Dat Ole un dat Nie Testament in unse Moderspraak
Vandenhoeck & Ruprecht, Göttingen,
4th edition 1968

[K1] Kaplan, R. W.: Der Ursprung des Lebens
dtv-Taschenbuch, 1972, 318 pages

[K2] Kemner, H.: Jesus trifft dich überall
Brunnen Publ. GmbH, Gießen and Basel 1971,
79 pages

[K3] Kemner, H.:      Gott baut auf allen Straßen
Brunnen Publ. GmbH, Gießen and Basel
2nd edition 1972, 87 pages

[K4] Kriese, R.:      Okkultismus im Angriff
Hänssler Publ., Neuhausen-Stuttgart
4th edition 1988, 224 pages

[K5] Kuberski, J.:      Eine 'Höllenfahrt Jesu'? – Zur Auslegung von
1. Petrus 3,18-20 –, Bibel und Gemeinde (1988),
H. 2, p. 181-197

[L1] LBS (Hrsg.):      Patentierte Lebensqualität von anno dazumal;
Ausgefallene Einfälle für besseres Bauen, mehr
Wohnkomfort, Sicherheit und leichteres Leben.
Zum Patent angemeldet 1877-1928. Brochure for
exhibition with the same name

[L2] Le Seur, P.:      Die Zukunft der Toten nach dem Sterben
Aussaat Publ., Wuppertal
10th edition 1976, 136 pages

[L3] Lewis, C. S.:      Grundsätze – Aphorismen und Gedanken
Brunnen Publ. GmbH, Basel and Gießen 1985,
79 pages

[O1] Oehlenschlä-
ger,D. (Hrsg.):      Mission – ein Lebenskonzept?
K. Lagershausen: Warum kommt ihr erst jetzt?
Brunnen Publ. GmbH, Gießen and Basel 1973,
70 pages

[O2] Ostermann, E.:      Das Glaubensbekenntnis der Evolution
Hänssler Publ., Neuhausen-Stuttgart 1978, 64 pages

[P1] Pache, R.:      Das Jenseits R. Brockhaus Publ., Wuppertal 1973,
224 pages

[P2] Padberg, L.V.:      Dialog zwischen Christentum und Weltreligionen
Bibel und Gemeinde 87 (1987), H. 1, p. 37-45

[P3] Pahls, W.:      Der große Unterschied zwischen Religion und
Evangelium, Evangelization sermon in a 2000- man
tent in Wienhausen near Celle on August 5, 1981

[R1] Richardson, D.:      Ewigkeit in ihren Herzen
Publ. of the Liebenzeller Mission, Bad Liebenzell,
1983, 240 pages

[R2] Ruhl, K. G:      Brauner Alltag
1933-1939 in Deutschland, Droste Verlag,
Düsseldorf, 1981, 167 pages

[S1] Sanders, J. O.:      Und die Menschen ohne Evangelium
Brunnen Publ. GmbH, Gießen and Basel
Überseeische Missionsgemeinschaft (ÜMG)
Zürich 2nd edition 1978, 87 pages

[S2]  Schirrmacher, T.:  Marxismus – Opium für das Volk?
                        Schwengeler Publ., Berneck 1990, 147 pages
[S3]  Schirrmacher, T.:  Die Religion des Nationalsozialismus
                        factum (1989), H. 11/12, p. 506-510
[S4]  Schirrmacher, T.:  Trinity in the Old Testament and Dialogue with the
                        Jews and Muslims
                        Calvinism Today (1991), Vol I, No. 1, p. 24-27
[S5]  Schirrmacher, T.:  Bibelkritik und Sünde oder: Der Sündenfall und
                        der Aufstand gegen den Schöpfer
                        Bibel und Gemeinde (1991), H. 2, p. 121-127
[S6]  Smith, O.:        Glühende Retterliebe
                        Publ. of the Schriftenmission der Ev. Gesellschaft
                        für Deutschland, Wuppertal-Elberfeld
                        10th edition 1972, 187 pages
[S7]  Spurgeon, C. H.:  Ganz aus Gnaden
                        J. G. Oncken Publ., Kassel
                        3rd edition 1965, 95 pages
[S8]  Spurgeon, C. H.:  Hast du mich lieb?
                        Christliche Literatur-Verbreitung, Bielefeld
                        3rd edition 1986, 287 pages
[T1]  Tanner, W.:       Altern und Tod aus der Sicht der Biologie
                        Biologie in unserer Zeit, 10(1980), p. 45-51
[U1]  Unfred, D.:       Evolution als Religion
                        factum (1985), H. 9, p. 12-14
[W1] Wagner, R.:        Novel "Ein Ende in Paris"
                        (Wagner über Beethoven, 1813-1883)
[W2] Wurmbrand, R.:     Erreichbare Höhen
                        Stephanus Edition, Seewis/Uhldingen
                        1st edition 1978, 464 pages

# Index of Authors

# List of Figures

# Abbreviations of the Books of the Bible

## Books of the Old Testament (OT)

| | | | |
|---|---|---|---|
| Genesis | Gen | Ecclesiaste | Eccl |
| Exodus | Ex | Song of Solomon | Song |
| Leviticus | Lev | Isaiah | Isaiah |
| Numbers | Num | Jeremiah | Jer |
| Deuteronomy | Deut | Lamentations | Lam |
| Joshua | Josh | Ezekiel | Ezek |
| Judges | Judg | Daniel | Dan |
| Ruth | Ruth | Hosea | Hosea |
| 1 Samuel | 1 Sam | Joel | Joel |
| 2 Samuel | 2 Sam | Amos | Amos |
| 1 Kings | 1 Kings | Obadiah | Obad |
| 2 Kings | 2 Kings | Jonah | Jonah |
| 1 Chronicles | 1 Chron | Micah | Micah |
| 2 Chronicles | 2 Chron | Nahum | Nahum |
| Ezra | Ezra | Habakkuk | Hab |
| Nehemiah | Neh | Zephaniah | Zeph |
| Esther | Esther | Haggai | Hag |
| Job | Job | Zechariah | Zech |
| Psalms | Ps | Malachi | Mal |
| Proverbs | Prov | | |

## Books of the New Testament (NT)

| | | | |
|---|---|---|---|
| Matthew | Matt | 1 Timothy | 1 Tim |
| Mark | Mark | 2 Timothy | 2 Tim |
| Luke | Luke | Titus | Titus |
| John | John | Philemon | Philem |
| The Acts | Acts | Hebrews | Hebr |
| Romans | Rom | James | James |
| 1 Corinthians | 1 Cor | 1 Peter | 1 Peter |
| 2 Corinthians | 2 Cor | 2 Peter | 2 Peter |
| Galatians | Gal | John 1 | John |
| Ephesians | Eph | 2John | 2 John |
| Philippians | Phil | 3 John | 3 John |
| Colossians | Col | Jude | Jude |
| 1 Thessalonians | 2 Thess | Revelation | Rev |
| 2 Thessalonians | 2 Thess | | |

Werner Gitt
# In the Beginning was Information

256 pages
ISBN 3-89397-252-2

Paperback

- The origin of life from the viewpoint of information science
- What is information?
- The origin of information
- Laws of nature about information
- Languages and communication
- Is artificial intelligence possible?

This are some topics of this interesting book about information, science and the Bible.

All living organisms require information to function. If we want to make meaningful and useful statements about the origin of life, then we first have to explain what information is and and how it came about. The author of this book uses many illustrative and striking examples to clarify this question.

The basic principles of information are clearly established in terms of laws and theorems which are just as valid and applicable as those employed in the natural sciences. The current materialistic representations of information are criticised, and an new model for the origin of live is derived.